Contents

Soho, 2007

IT WAS LATE on a warm summer night and the centre of London was buzzing. Tourists, partygoers, and home-grown Londoners were out and about, having a late night drink in a bar, returning to their homes or hotels, or just hanging out on the street. But suddenly, the sound of screaming filled the air. Startled onlookers were stunned to see one of the most famous singers in the country sprinting through the streets, covered in blood and bandages, drunk, stoned, and in a terrible mess.

Amy Winehouse was in trouble. In just three short years, she'd rocketed from complete unknown to mega star. Her extraordinary voice and song writing talents looked set to propel her to the very top of the music world: she was globally famous, sought after all over the world, and looked to be one of the very few British stars who was actually going to crack the United States. But as her star rose, her personal problems rocketed. A self-confessed heavy drinker and dope smoker, Amy had by now graduated to hard drugs, with disastrous effect. Her weight had plummeted and her body was covered with gashes and scars, a result of cutting herself repeatedly. She was in a terrible state.

As she ran through Soho, the man many blamed for her problems, her husband Blake, pursued her. The two had married in a surprise ceremony only a couple of months previously and their union was as tempestuous as it was passionate. 'Amy! Amy!' screamed Blake as he tore through the streets after her, only for his wife to flag down a passing car and leap in, leaving Blake screaming on the street after her. The two were clearly on the verge of collapse.

But even this was not the lowest point of Amy's life to date. Just a few weeks earlier, she'd been treated for a near-fatal drugs overdose and she and Blake had been playing out their very fiery relationship in public, frequently seen covered in blood and bruises and high on drugs. However, crunch time was approaching. Amy was due to kick off a tour in the autumn; Blake, meanwhile, was on his way to jail.

In the event, the tour was abandoned halfway through as Amy, more fragile than ever, struggled vainly to cope. She had already amassed huge amounts of public goodwill: the combination of her talent and vulnerability had aroused a great deal of sympathy and concern. She was often com-pared to Billie Holliday, Judy Garland – all the greats. But they all had one thing in common: a massive self-destructive streak that took them to an early grave. Would Amy have a career as great as any of theirs – and still survive?

When Amy Jade Winehouse was born on 14 September 1983 – four years after her brother Alex, to Mitchell, a taxi driver, and Janis, who went on to become a pharmacist – no one had a clue what lay ahead. The Winehouse family came from a respectable, middle-class Jewish background. Her father Mitch later recalled, 'We would go to my mum's every Friday for dinner. She would say, "Get in the kitchen, Amy, and serve the guests." It was all designed to keep her feet on the ground. Her second album was a tribute to her grandmother.' Indeed, Amy adored Mitch's mother Cynthia: one of her tattoos, the name Cynthia above the figure of a glamour model, was in honour of her her.

It was a modest childhood. The family was comfortable, but not extravagant, and holidays were spent either in England or Spain. 'I love Southend – it's just the classic English seaside,' said Amy. 'I spent a lot of time there when I was growing up because I had family there and I love going to the airshow. Marbella is my earliest memory of being on holiday – I must have been about two years old. I had a dolls' house and remember my brother and me playing with it on the beach. We didn't travel much when I was a kid – it was mainly big family holidays to Spain with my nan.'

The first real drama in Amy's life came when she was nine, when her father walked out. Many close friends and family believe that was the start of her destructive streak, although Amy herself played it down.

'My childhood was really good,' she said. 'We lived in a semi-detached house down the road from my gran. My dad left when I was nine. They sat us down and said, "We're separating". It was all very open. I think it hit my brother worse. All I knew was that it meant I could wear make-up, short skirts, and swear at my mum. I didn't mind dad going because I thought it would be fun and I knew he wouldn't disappear, he'd always be there.'

It was not, however, quite as simple as that. It was not always obvious whether Mitch was in gainful employment, and if he was, what, exactly, he was doing. His own life was peripatetic in the extreme: 'He moved every two years,' Amy once revealed. 'I've no idea what he was trying to run from.'

It was also – she revealed much, much, later – a time when she began to self-harm. In recent years Amy has been seen in public with a fair number of gashes on her arm, but this actually began well over a decade previously. 'It's a funny thing, a morbid curiosity,' she said. 'I'm talking about when I was nine. What does that feel like? "Ow, that fucking hurts." It's probably the worst thing I've done.'

From then on, as Amy relates it, she and her brother were left to compete for the attention of the older, female members of her family, not least her grandmother who, said Amy, is 'redoubtable,' 'frank', and has been sixty-two 'for at least sixteen years.'

She was not, however always the easiest of daughters, and with no father around to restrain her, did sometimes get out of control. 'I feel very bad about the way I was to my mum,' Amy has admitted. 'I was such a terrible child because she was there and my dad wasn't. I think we blamed her in a small way, probably more me because I'm a real daddy's girl. Not out and out like, "It's your fault he's gone!" Just being really horrible. I never used to be, like, "When's daddy coming home?" I was a mean little shit and when my dad left I could do what I wanted.'

One person who did manage to keep her under control was her grandmother, Cynthia, with whom Amy had a special bond. She managed to calm her excesses: 'Amy was always a tearaway but Cynthia helped keep her on the straight and narrow,' said a family friend.

Although she knew pretty much from the word go what she wanted to do, that didn't stop Amy from wondering about the future in the way little girls do. 'When I was a child I wanted to be a lab technician (like my mum), a dancer (just because kids do), a journalist (I was one for a couple of years, too),' she confided in later years. 'I wish I'd never worn the stuff my dad used to dress me in when I was little. I hated it. He once bought my brother and me matching gloves, hats and berets with woolly rosettes on them. He thought we looked great – I can assure you we didn't.'

She was nothing if not a precocious child. Amy was brought up listening to jazz: her parents adored Frank Sinatra, Dinah Washington, and Ella Fitzgerald; her uncles were professional jazz musicians; and her grandmother had once gone out with Ronnie Scott. 'She wouldn't have sex with him until they married, and he wanted to marry her, but wouldn't unless they had sex before – 'cos he didn't know whether he would enjoy himself. So he went off,' Amy explained.

Music was everywhere: 'With my schoolfriends, I listened to hiphop and Missy Elliott,' she says, 'but jazz was my private thing. From the age of eleven I loved it.' It was clearly what she was going to want to do. 'There was always music on in my house when I was growing up,' she said. 'Dad liked people like Sarah Vaughan and mum listened to Carole King. I knew music was what I wanted to do. I would sing in my bedroom and stuff like that.'

But it took her a little while to do so publicly. 'As a little kid I was too shy to sing and my brother was the one standing on a chair in his school uniform and doing his Frank Sinatra,' she told one interviewer, pointing to a picture of him. 'That's him holding my Cabbage Patch doll to ransom. Then eventually, when I was about nine, I did it. "Sing!" my nana would shout. "And smile!" But I still needed to hold a fan to my face for "Eternal Flame": "Close your eyes, give me your hand ..."'

Against that background, it was almost inevitable that Amy would become involved with music, and she did. When she was just ten, Amy and her closest friend, Juliette Ashby, formed a rap duo called Sweet 'n' Sour, which was based on Salt 'n' Pepa. It was one of her rare brushes with pop music.

'No, never,' she said, when asked if she'd ever been a big pop fan, 'apart from when I was six or seven, when I liked Kylie and loved Madonna. I listened to Madonna's *Immaculate Collection* every day until I was about eleven, and then I discovered Salt 'n' Pepa and TLC. That was, "Oh my God. This is my music!" My best friend Juliette and me started our first ever band, Sweet 'n' Sour. We were rappers. I was Sour, of course.'

Juliette remained Amy's closest friend as an adult, and the two of them liked to reminisce about their childhood together. 'We met at Osidge when we were about four,' Amy recalled. 'One of my first memories is that we'd play this game where Juliette was Pepsi and I was Shirley, the backing girls for Wham! I think we clicked because we were both a bit off-key.'

'A bit nutty. And we were always in trouble,' Juliette added.

'You'd get sent to the school reception if you were naughty and we were always meeting up there,' Amy continued. 'We told this boy, Ian Beerman, that if he didn't pull his pants down we wouldn't be his friends any more. And he did it.'

'That was when we truly bonded,' Juliette confirmed. 'I used to egg Amy on a bit more because she was more fearless. One of our best routines was that one of us would run out of the classroom in tears, and the other would say that they'd have to go out and comfort her. And then we'd just sit in a room somewhere, laughing for the rest of the lesson.'

A year later, now at state secondary school Ashmole in Southgate, she was playing the guitar. A year after that, she won a scholarship to the Sylvia Young Theatre School – although she lasted just three years.

It was when she was thirteen that Amy really started to rebel. A pupil at the Sylvia Young Stage School (one of her classmates was Billie Piper), Amy stood out even amongst her energetic schoolmates. Her headmaster was becoming increasingly upset by her activities: her 'desecration' of her school uniform, and also what he saw as her 'lack of application'. Finally, one day she went too far and turned up for school with a nose stud (she'd pierced her nose herself). 'I was expelled,' she explained. Her first tattoo followed shortly afterwards. And what did her parents make of it? 'My parents pretty much realised I would do what I wanted and that was it, really.'

And she took a while to blossom. 'She never went to stage school for the singing, she went for the acting and dancing,' her father Mitch later recalled. 'Jane [his second wife] and I went to see her sing when she was twelve or thirteen and it wasn't very good. A year later she invited us to this musical she was in and we thought, "Oh no". But suddenly her singing was really great. I don't know where it comes from. I love to sing and I love jazz. But her mum's side of the family is the musical one. A couple of her uncles were professional musicians.'

Sylvia Young Theatre School, while not ultimately the place that was going to introduce Amy to the world, did at least understand that she had a real talent. 'They had us singing "Flashdance" and all stuff from musicals, "Where Is Love", cheesy stuff like that,' Amy said. 'But if we ever had a jazzy song or a sexy, husky song they'd always give me a solo in that.'

But she didn't fit in. 'I got kicked out because I got a nose ring,' she said, on another occasion. 'The other schools I had to leave because of repeated bad behaviour. I didn't like school and thought I was smarter than most of the teachers.' Nor was she mad keen on her fellow students. 'I wasn't gregarious,' she said. 'There were lots of totally insufferable kids there who'd come into class and announce, "My mummy's coming to pick me up for an audition at three o'clock". I was a little weirdo, I suppose, in that young, random way, but I wasn't a loner. Friends would go, "Come and be weird with us!"'

On another occasion, Amy herself talked about her experiences rather differently. 'When I left Sylvia Young, I hated school so much that I didn't want to go at all,' she said. 'That was horrid. I was gutted when I left, because there are some really dedicated people there, and Sylvia herself is brilliant. I pierced my nose when I was thirteen. They didn't like that. I brought my guitar to school every day because I was a guitarist and they'd tell me I couldn't. I was like, "Well, look, I'm a singer, a musician, not an academic..." But that's what made me a better person, it showed me that you can't be taught stuff; you have to go out there and find out for yourself.'

Amy began to realize that she might actually be able to do this for a living. 'I mean, I knew I could get a bit of money out of it doing stuff on stage, in a chorus line or whatever,' she said. 'But I thought everyone could sing. I didn't think it was a skill. It was only when my mum said "You know, you've got something special there" that I took it seriously.'

After she left, Amy was sent to the £3,000-a-term Mount School in Mill Hill, a short distance from where the family lived in Southgate, North London, where she took five GCSEs. Her English teacher at the time, Christine Hughes, also felt she was beginning to take an interest in her own image. 'Amy came across as very domineering, but I also felt she wanted to have more street cred and played down her own upbringing, which I think was quite privileged. She always knew exactly what she wanted and well done to her for getting so far.'

For Amy, however, the school was a miserable experience. 'It was horrific,' she said. 'Disgusting. Girls are fucking mad. There's a reason why I didn't want to go to a school without any boys and that's because girls are just weird. They are so weird. You know how women go, "Men are so weird, I don't understand them" and tell their mums, who say, "You never will, dear"? Well, I don't agree with that, I think it's the other way round. Girls are mad. They were just backwards. You need men there. I ended up running the school. There were only two girls I liked: all the rest of them were scared of us. They would try to talk to us and we'd be like, "fuck off".'

Amy then went on to the BRIT Performing Arts and Technology School in Croydon, before doing a number of dead end jobs, including one in a piercing parlour: 'That was so gross,' she said afterwards. 'Piercing people's ears isn't too bad, but their noses? Bleurgh!' There followed a short-lived flirtation with music journalism with the show business WENN news network, where the change in her image continued. 'Amy is basically a nice girl from North London who has a major talent,' said a colleague from those days. 'I heard her on the radio the other day and she sound-ed a lot like the rebel type who hangs around in Camden Market, which isn't what her background was about at all.'

Amy was a typical teenager in other ways: running around town, enjoying herself, and learning about gigs and the music of the day. But there was a hint of problems in the future when she related the first time she'd been to Brixton Academy, and the first time she saw Erykah Badu: as she was to do so many times in the future, she started to have a problem with food.

'So excited was I, in fact, that I didn't eat all day and got told off by a friend,' she recalled. 'Then, at the gig, I passed out, which I'd never done before or since. I still remember people milling around me, and my friend, Nicky, having to pull my tongue out of my mouth, just in case I choked. Then a security guy carried me to the sick bay, where this St John's adolescent was holding up my legs to try to get the blood back into my cheeks. Which wasn't funny: I was wearing a short skirt.' She survived to tell the tale, but it was clear her problems dated from a long way back.

Amy wasn't really cut out for music journalism: she didn't enjoy it, and began writing songs and singing with the National Youth Jazz Orchestra instead. It was at this point that a friend, Nick Shymansky, heard her singing and was so impressed he gave her studio time to record some demos.

It was her great good fortune, however, that her demo was passed to a record company employee, at which point, aged just sixteen, the management company 19 – which was run by Simon Fuller (who was responsible for the Spice Girls) – began pursuing her. Initially, Amy turned them down, convinced they were going to try to make her into a pop star.

'I was a tunnel vision teenager,' she said. 'I knew what I wanted to do and I didn't believe them when they said, "We're not gonna pop you up."'

But 19 persevered and, after a year, they finally signed

her. A record contract with Universal Island followed when she was eighteen, along with a link-up with Salaam Remi, who was Ms Dynamite's producer. It was the right person at the right time. Norah Jones was making jazz-cum-blues a massively popular area, and Amy was happy to acknowledge the debt she had to her. 'I think, with any musician, you take in as much as you can of all these different influences, and when it comes out it's unique, because it's filtered through you,' she said.

Meanwhile, the friendship with Juliette continued. Amy had by now left home, and the two of them rented a flat together, where all manner of bad behaviour went on. 'We always met at my house when we got to about sixteen and started smoking dope, and when I got my publishing deal at eighteen the first thing I did after I signed the contract and got my advance was to get a flat with Juliette,' Amy recalled.

'I've got such brilliant memories of that flat,' said Juliette. 'I'd have passed out from being stoned, and Amy would be roasting a chicken at three in the morning. When she's stressed, or a bit fucked up in the head, Amy'll be in the kitchen. She loves feeding people. She's a nutcase, but she's a good person. I worry for her a lot. There have been nights when I've been in bed and I've heard this banging sound.'

'And it's been me, banging my head against the wall,' Amy put in. 'I don't do that so much these days.'

The friendship was certainly a strong one. 'We both know that we'd rescue each other from a burning building if we had to,' said Juliette. 'We've got that understanding. You can rely on your friends to be there when your family has totally washed their hands of you. I mean, we still share a house after all this time. In fact, I always said that if Amy were a black man, we'd be married. We're that close.'

Amy was now gearing up to hit the music scene. Her debut single, 'Stronger Than Me', caused some ripples, attacking, as it did, an ex-boyfriend for being sissy.

It was around this time that the buzz really started to spread about Amy. She supported Jamie Cullum on a UK tour, and began to understand the places in which she liked to perform. 'I like a small gig, and to be able to see everyone in the audience. That's where I'm coming from,' she said.

Amy burst suddenly into the public consciousness with her first album, *Frank*, in part a reference to her own frankness within her songs, but also an homage to her father's hero, Frank Sinatra. 'Sinatra was an arsehole, I do understand that, but he had something, this connection to the songs,' she says.

Frank, the album, was also about an ex-boyfriend. 'I'm

hard on him but I'm hard on myself, too,' said Amy. 'The last time I spoke to him, he said, "Send me an album." I said to him, "Do me a favour! I don't even have a copy myself, so what am I supposed to send you?" So he said, "Go in the shop and buy me one." And I said, "Why?" And he goes, "Because I'm too embarrassed. I can't go in the shop and buy an album that is about me." And I'm like, "Yeah, but people don't know you! If I go in a shop, they'd be like, "You're buying your own album, you sad bitch!" Yaknowwotamean!?! And he said to me, "Look, I've got to see you, I owe you a tenner, so why don't you just give me an album when I see you." I said, "I'll tell you what, why don't you keep the tenner, let's not see each other, just go and buy the album for fuck's sake!"'

Her father was also taking an interest in her music, something Amy felt a little dubious about. 'My dad sings my songs all the time,' she said. 'The songs are very intimate to me, but I've had to say to myself, they're out of me now, they're in the world, anyone can hear them. But it's still embarrassing when your dad sings all the risque lines and goes, "You meant that in the rude way, didn't you? You're terrible, Amy." And I'm like, "Oh my God, someone kill me!"'

The single attracted immediate attention and with it, rumours that Amy, if not yet allowing herself to be pushed by Fuller into a more poppy style, might do so in the future. 'I'm not worried,' she said. 'I've met him twice. My A&R man is paranoid about it because he doesn't want people to think he [Fuller] did it. I'll tell you what people should worry about. The fact that Simon, when S Club started fucking up ... he replaced them. SClub 7, SClub 8... it's all the same. Now that's fucked. He's mad, that Simon Fuller. I don't think he cares if he gets a return on me. He's got *Pop Idol* and his empire. He's a smart man, and he's clever enough to know he can't fuck with me.'

She was only that overprotective about her music, however, and surprisingly pragmatic (and honest) about other things. 'Everything can be improved on,' she said. 'I'm not so proud as a woman that I'd say, "No! I'll never get my breasts done!" Fuck it. I probably would, when I'm old and whatever. I'm a girly girl. It's just my music. It's the only thing I have real dignity in, in my life. That's the one area in my life where I can hold my head up and say, "No one can touch me." 'Cos no one can touch me!'

Another noteworthy song was, 'What Is It About Men?', which was quite clearly about Mitch and his girlfriends. Amy conceded as much. 'It's me trying to work out my dad's problems with sticking with one woman, trying to make sense of why he did certain things,' she said. 'I completely understand it now. People like to have sex with people. I

23

don't begrudge my dad just because he has a penis. What's the point?'

Mitch himself took it on the chin. 'I think it's only the first part that's specifically about me,' he said. 'The rest of it is more generally about what rats men are. But the song's given me pause for thought, because the divorce obviously coloured her view of men.'

And then there was, 'I Heard Love Is Blind', in which Amy describes a one night stand, which was acceptable because the man involved resembled her boyfriend: 'Just not as tall but I couldn't tell/ It was dark and I was lying down.'

'That's life, innit?' said Amy unrepentantly. 'And that's the sort of thing a man would say. "I slept with this girl, she was blonde like you, and she had this bit at the front of her hair like you, but baby it didn't mean anything.' Ha ha. So there was a bit of role-reversal going on there. The gay thing [in 'Stronger Than Me'] was me just wanting some affection. It's not like I need to be the centre of attention all the time. But if my man comes round and turns on the TV, unless it's football I'm like, "Are you even attracted to me?"'

It was an incredibly sassy debut and happened in a very short time. But Amy was still extremely young, prone to self-destructive behaviour and totally unprepared for the pressures that being in the limelight would bring. She badly needed stability in her life, but seemed to be attracted to quite the opposite: bad boys who brought with them only chaos and pain. Amy's slightly fractured childhood had left more scars than she cared to admit, and while her song writing was a way of dealing with them, it also opened her vulnerabilities up to the world. Not that that mattered to Amy ... to begin with at least: she loved being a star.

But the early success of *Frank* was as nothing compared to what awaited her. Her second album, *Back to Black*, was to catapult her into the major league, with all the trials and tribulations that it brings in its wake. For Amy, a tumultuous time lay ahead.

A Star Is Born

IT HAD BEEN a sensational debut. Not only had Amy's first album, *Frank*, sold 200,000 copies, but she was up for two Brit awards: Best British Female and Best Urban Act. Amy, as ever, was playing it cool. 'I remember that awful boy band A1 winning best newcomers so maybe it will be a blessing if it doesn't happen,' she remarked at the Brit Nomination launch party at London's Park Lane Hotel.

She was clearly thrilled, of course, but she did manage to keep her feet on the ground. 'I'm not a great singer, yaknowotamean?' she said in an early interview. 'People are very throwaway with their words these days. If someone comes out and they've got hoop earrings and a big bum, it's like, "She's a diva!" You have to earn these things. Not from other people, from yourself. You have to earn your own respect. [But] it's very flattering to be acknowledged, and especially to be put with the women as opposed to the new artists. I feel like I've jumped a step. But it's Dido's award, really, isn't it? She has to get it so everyone can kind of justify why they bought her album.'

Amy was also making a fair few admirers within the industry, as she was clearly not letting it all go to her head. 'I've been very lucky with the record deal and the beautiful blessings that came with it, but I want more from life than people knowing who I am,' she said. 'I'm not the girl who worked and dreamt the hardest. I'm just a musician who put some songs together. That's all I ever wanted to do, although it was a bit too straight for me. But, if my career should die right now, I would go to Vegas and be a lounge singer, do that every night for the rest of my life, and I would be completely happy, yaknowwotamean?'

Indeed, she gave every indication that she was as surprised by it all as anyone. On the eve of a short UK tour, which was beginning in Manchester, she sounded quite surprised at her own luck. 'I wasn't expecting those nominations,' she said. 'I just want respect from other musicians. Fame isn't something I've shopped for. I don't even see myself as a singer. I'm a musician. The thing I've always prided myself on is that I don't sound like anyone else. I'm not saying I'm a brilliant vocalist – but I am different.'

Her astonishing openness was also winning her fans. Asked if future boyfriends might be a little cautious with her given that the last one featured so heavily on *Frank*, she replied, 'Yeah, I'm an open book. Some men do think I'm a psycho bunny-boiler. But I think that's funny. If you're nice to me I'll never write anything bad about you. There's no point in saying anything but the truth. Because, at the end of the day, I don't have to answer to you, or my ex, or ... I shouldn't say God ... or a man in a suit from the record company. I have to answer to myself.'

She certainly wasn't worried about answering to the record company. When it came to being outspoken, Amy could not be outdone. 'Some things on this album make me go to a little place that's fucking bitter,' she said of record company interference. 'I've never heard the album from start to finish. I don't have it in my house. Well, the marketing was fucked and the promotion was terrible. Everything was a shambles. It's frustrating, because you work with so many idiots – but they're nice idiots. So you can't be like, "You're an idiot." I've not seen anyone from the record company since the album came out and I know why: 'cos they're scared of me. They know I have no respect for them whatsoever. Look, I know it's a terrible thing for someone to come out and say they hate their own music. It's the worst thing you can do. My album isn't shit. If I heard someone else singing like me I would buy it in a heartbeat.'

On another occasion she remarked, 'I dunno, I'm a young girl or I was at one point, especially when I was writing those songs, and I just write the way I talk and the way I think about things and my perspectives. I would never put in a lyric just because I think "ooh, that would sound nice, the way the words fall" ... well, I do do that, but it has to have content, you know what I mean? It's important to me to challenge myself.'

In the event of her not winning a Brit, Amy seemed determined to get her retaliation in first. 'I don't recognise the Brit Awards; it is not a worthwhile award to have,' she said on the eve of the awards. 'I know that is the worst thing to say but I am so sure I am not going to get one I really don't give a shit.' She also had a pop at the woman who did eventually win. Of Dido she said, 'She's bland. Her songs aren't thought out, her lyrics aren't thought out, her voice isn't thought out. It's background music – the background to death.' Even though Amy lost out to Dido as Best British Female Solo Artist, she was on her way. Just days later, she was nominated for another award: Best Contemporary Song for 'Stronger Than Me' at the Ivor Novello Awards.

Amy, still only twenty, had turned overnight from un-known into superstar and yet still she kept her head. 'It's cool,' she said. 'My life isn't really different to how it used to be. It's better in that I'm working more now. You know how when you don't go to work, you don't always feel one hundred per cent? Well, because I'm working a lot, I feel like I'm doing good things now.'

She was also intensely relieved she hadn't done what so many aspiring singers do: try to get on a programme such as *Pop Idol*. 'I never wanted any of this and that's the truth,' she said. 'I would have been happy to sing in a cov-ers band for the rest of my life. And I wouldn't have gone on one of those shows in a million, billion years, because I think that musicality is not something other people should judge you on. Music's a thing you have with yourself. Even though the people who go on those shows are shit, it's really damaging to be told that you are.'

In her effort to maintain true to herself, the only thing Amy allowed her record company to control was her im-age. But even here, she soon took over herself. 'Well, for a while it was looking like they were going to style me,' she said in an interview at the time. 'Recently, when things started getting busy, they started trussing me up. The thing about me is I'm edgier than that – if you make me up too much I end up looking like someone's auntie. I've had to reclaim my own look.'

'I've given them a lot of control. I made the music be-cause I know how to do that, but then for the promotional side I stepped back and thought, "I've got to trust this lot, because I've never done this before". That was the wrong thing to do. All they know how to do is what's already been done and I don't want to do anything that's already been done. I don't ever want to do anything mediocre. I hear the music in the charts and I don't mean to be rude, but those people have no soul. Learning from music is like eating a meal – you have to pace yourself. You can't take everything from it all at once. I want to be different, definitely. I'm not a one-trick pony. I'm at least a five-trick pony.'

As for the future, Amy was happy to think about settling down. 'Well, I'll have at least three beautiful kids,' she said. 'I want to do at least four or five albums and I want to get them out of the way now. And then I want to take ten years out to go and have kids, definitely. I never used to be broody, but then I realised that I'm turning into a soppy bitch. Goodness in life comes from a sense of achievement, and you'd get that from having a child and putting it before yourself.'

But despite her Jewish background, she did not, she said, have faith. 'I'm not religious at all. I think faith is something that gives you strength. I believe in fate and I believe that things happen for a reason but I don't think that there's a high power, necessarily. I believe in karma very much though. There are so many rude people around and they're the people that don't have any real friends. And relationships with people – with your mum, your nan, your dog – are what you get the most happiness in life from. Apart from shoes and bags.'

Amy was still shapely at that time, but by June 2004, the first signs of what would grow to become extremely big problems in the future became apparent. She pulled out of the press launch of a concert at the last minute blaming illness, but it seems that something quite different was wrong. 'She drank too much beer at a gig the night before and was too ill to attend,' said a source. At the time everyone just put it down to youthful high spirits – after all, she was on a roll – but this was the first sign of a problem that would threaten to get out of control.

There was another hiccup shortly afterwards. Amy performed at a VIP bash in London's Old Street for the phone giant T-Mobile, where she performed some new songs. Unfortunately, it appeared that she hadn't actually learned them yet. 'Amy had trouble remembering the lyrics. She actually said, "I have to try to remember this shit now,"' said a guest at the gig. 'That's not exactly a very good plug for her new material.' There was no suggestion that Amy was out of control on the night in question, but it was a sign of erratic behaviour that was going to get worse as time went on.

Not that it seemed to worry Amy in the least. She rounded on her fellow singers again, staring with the doyenne of them all, Madonna. 'She's an old lady. She can't shock any more. She should get a nice band, just stand in front of them and fucking sing,' Winehouse proclaimed.

She then turned her attention to Chris Martin of Coldplay. 'I bet if he heard his stuff he'd be like, "Who is that wanker?"'

Katie Melua? 'She's shit.'

And the cause for Amy's attitude to all these highly successful people? 'I'm slightly bitter because I haven't sold as many albums as them.'

And that, of course, was how Amy managed to get away with it: underneath it all, she could laugh at herself, which let her off the hook elsewhere. She was also learning to play the game. Attacking her fellow stars attracted a lot of publicity, which is exactly what an up-and-coming chanteuse like Amy needed: it was a very competitive world out there and she was determined to win. And she was doing very well. In July, she was shortlisted for the prestigious Mercury Prize and shortly afterwards made a hugely successful appearance at the JJB Arena. Again, she didn't win the Mercury, losing out to Franz Ferdinand, but again – it didn't matter.

She was also showing that no one could boss her around. 'For the "In My Bed" video, I had on a little tiny pink D&G dress, and the woman at the record company handed me a long, knee-length red dress,' she related. 'I was like, "No, no, no, dear. I can't even walk in this dress. I always wear what I want to wear."'

More ominously, given what was to come, Amy was also keen to talk about her enjoyment of marijuana. 'I have smoked an ounce a week at times,' she said. 'When I smoke, I am just the happy me. I sing or whistle for three hours or go up and play guitar for four hours. I like a drink. I love all different kinds of alcohol and, everywhere I go, I'll find a drink I like. But I am more of a smoker. All my inhibitions go, so it's great to write when I'm stoned.'

She was also beginning to quantify herself as an artist. 'I sing better onstage than on record,' she said. 'If you see me, I'll do crazy stuff that will get your hair standing up. I don't pride myself on being technically perfect. I'm a feeling singer, but if I crack I will always come back.'

Such was Amy's success by this time that observers of the music industry were beginning to talk about a new 'jazz age'. After all, Amy wasn't the only singer to be performing in a brand new style (or rather, an older style than those that had recently been more popular): others included Jamie Cullum and Katie Melua. She may have been incredibly talented, but she was also in the right place at the right time.

But at that stage she was riding high. Her name was now widely known and when it was announced she was to play at the Pizza Express Jazz Club in Soho, the tickets promptly sold out. Her personal life was also running relatively smoothly: she was now ensconced with Tyler James, another singer. The two lived together in a chaotic flat in Camden, where Amy's more domestic side could be on display: cooking, when she was in the mood, and playing with the neighbour's cats, even if one interviewer did describe the flat as looking like a crime scene because of the mess. However, the warning signs, as she recounted it to one newspaper, were already there.

'I don't have any food in my fridge,' she declared. 'I'm working all the time promoting my album, *Frank*, so I don't have much chance to get food in. But you know what? I did go out yesterday to get unsmoked bacon and free-range eggs for breakfast because I would have been shouted at if I hadn't. My boyfriend Tyler got me into bacon and egg sandwiches for breakfast; either of us will make them depending on who gets out of bed first. I'll probably have Jack Daniel's and Coke next. The quantity I drink depends on how much I've got in the house left over from the night before. Tyler has just brought me a massive bottle from Monaco, so I'm all right at the moment.'

It was all very rock 'n' roll (or rock 'n' jazz), but as anyone could have told her, that kind of lifestyle was going to land Amy in serious trouble. But no one did tell her, or if they did, she didn't listen. She was still maintaining a normal weight, and so perhaps public confessions about persistent use of marijuana and Jack Daniels for breakfast didn't ring the alarm bells they should. And according to Amy, she was eating a relatively healthy diet – drinking aside.

'When I'm at home alone for dinner I'll put on roast chicken and have it with vegetables and, if I'm with Tyler or someone, I'll cook potatoes with it,' she continued. 'I don't eat much stodge. I've never done the Atkins diet but, before it became really popular, I knew that bread, rice, pasta, and potato made you fat. I cut them out for about eight months but that was about five years ago. I eat for England now. I eat and eat and eat. I love food; I think eating is fun. Luckily my voice doesn't get affected by food – unless I've got my mouth full.' It was not, unfortunately, an attitude she was able to maintain.

In early 2007, it was announced that Amy was going to appear in the Prince's Trust concert to be held in May. Another appearance was at London's Barbican with Neneh Cherry and Fontella Bass in *Billie and Me*, featuring the music of Billie Holliday. She won a great deal of praise for her appearance, with one critic noting that she looked more relaxed that night than she did at her own concerts.

She continued to be outspoken, amusing people with her account of appearing with Jonathan Ross on radio and

TV: 'I went on his radio show the day after I was on his TV show,' she said, 'and when I walked in, he had a lovely suit on and I said, "You look so smart". He said, "I'm always smart!" and I went, "Well you looked like a schmuck yesterday!"'

Amy's own style was becoming increasingly distinctive. Asked about her beauty secrets in an interview, she replied, 'Crystal Clear facials', before going on to reveal that the contents of her make-up bag were Paul & Joe foundation and coral lipstick, mascara, eyeliner, and red lipliner, although in truth, anyone looking at her would have been able to work that out. 'My friends say I can't dress, but I'd just say that I'm quite eclectic,' she continued, citing the 1940s as the best era for clothes. 'I love those seamed stockings, that beautiful silhouette, and the hairstyles and make-up,' she said.

But still the warning note continued to ring. In the same interview, she revealed that her idea of bliss was, 'To start working really early in the day and be finished by 3pm – then home to watch The *Fresh Prince of Bel Air* on television with a fat spliff and a Jack Daniels.' No one picked up on the warning signs – indeed, it was all grist to the mill for Amy's image. The wild image went with the wild voice and the increasingly wild appearance, although the dramatic weight loss and the tattoos were still some way off.

People certainly were fascinated by this Betty Boop-ish figure that had seemingly sprung out of nowhere. Another paper asked her to recount her five favourite things. The first was *The Fresh Prince of Bel Air*: 'I don't really watch much TV, but I love this show. It's funny. I remember splitting up with my boyfriend a few years ago and the only thing I could get out of bed for was the show.' (This, incidentally, was another hint of Amy's depressive streak.) Another was cats: 'They come into the house because I live in a courtyard and there are always some around. I love to bring them in.' Amy other favourite things were a guitar called the Gretch White Falcon, the author Elmore Leonard, and, perhaps inevitably, Jack Daniels.

Amy was also keen to avoid being put into an 'easy listening' slot in the nation's psyche. 'I would say that I don't rest in that category,' she said. 'Katie Melua is easy listening, and I wouldn't say that my music is. I dance to hip-hop and listen to it when I'm at home. But when I'm alone and there's no one else around, I'll listen to more personal music. You can have the music on, chill out and not give a fuck about anything. That's when you'd put on my album. I see my album as a night album, or a morning album. It's not a during-the-day album.'

Meanwhile, battles with her publicity people continued, as they tried to control her image. Amy was having none of it. 'Sometimes they'll tell me I can't wear stuff because it's too sexy and I'm like, "Fuck off, I'd wear this out, so I'll wear it today, 'cos that's what I would be wearing if I didn't have to come and do shit for you". I'm not going to wear something outrageous for the sake of it. I want to wear what I want to wear, and what will look good and appropriate.'

Amy was becoming increasingly self-analytical about what she did. People were intrigued to hear such an old voice from such a young mouth, especially one with such insight. And Amy's own ambitions were undergoing a sea change. 'When I was younger I wanted to be in musicals,' she said. 'That's something I could never do now, but all those songs from the shows, those pure, simple, beautiful songs – I loved them. And from there I got into jazz.'

Asked about whether jazz was not a bit old for her, she replied, 'Well, it is old music. It's also excluding music. At jazz gigs, everyone's got their eyes closed or they're studying the soloist really intently. If you don't like hip hop, you can still go to a hip hop gig and get off on the girls dancing with each other, everyone waving their drinks in the air, and passing joints around – it's a nice vibe. I'm trying to mix up the styles, which is why I don't sing standards. I'm taking old music and trying to make something new. Maybe I'll sing covers when I'm older, but I'm young and I want to write songs about my life now.'

With Amy's growing popularity came an increasing clamour to see her on stage. In April 2004, she made her debut in Scotland, at Glasgow's Cottier Theatre, with Tyler coming on first as her supporting act.

She certainly wasn't shy about blowing her own trumpet, and was becoming increasingly tetchy about comparisons with her peers, such as Katie Melua, Jamie Cullum, and Norah Jones. 'I think that as my output increases people will realise that I'm in a class of my own,' she said coolly. 'I'm different. I don't pride myself on being a great singer; I pride myself on being unique and on writing music that I would like to hear. That is what drives me. I don't mind being lumped next to people like Jamie, but the rest of them aren't even musicians. However much I know that she's shit, there are people that think Katie Melua is a real musician. That really gets to me.'

She was equally scathing when it came to Simon Fuller – who was, after all, her manager – and her record company, which had forced some changes to her album. Asked what she thought of Fuller, she replied, 'I don't know. I've only met him twice. Business people don't leave an impression with me. They go out of my head straight away.'

As for her record label – 'I made my album and then

they did what they wanted to it,' she said. 'They don't talk to me like I'm a person; they talk to me like I'm a product. If they've got a problem with the way my music sounds or with me, I couldn't care less. They couldn't say anything to me that I haven't said to myself. I'm my own biggest critic.' And as for her next album: 'I'd do it from home for a start,' she declared. Even for someone known for her outspokenness, it was pretty gutsy stuff. And it was just the beginning.

Darkness Falls

AMY MIGHT have been blasé about awards – or at least, she said she was – but it wasn't long before another one was on the cards. She was nominated in the highly prestigious Ivor Novello awards, in the Best Contemporary Song category for 'Stronger Than Me', up against the likes of Dizzee Rascal and Kylie Minogue. It was heady stuff.

Meanwhile, Amy was beginning to relax a little more when it came to her live performances. Her reviewers had always noted the power of her voice: it was merely a case of nerves that had been criticised in the past. Now she was beginning to come into her own, with one reviewer commenting on the enormous energy and spirit she was putting into her live performances. Opinions were united: this was a massive star on the rise.

Her home life, however, was rather more complicated. Amy confessed that Tyler was not the only man on the scene: 'I'm seeing a couple of people,' she said. 'Seeing one person is not important. It's just like, you get home and you smoke a joint. When you get home, you smoke a joint. No,

I can't explain it. At the end of your day, call a man, get a man round, bang, that's it.'

While that may have marked Amy out as unconventional, it did hint at something else, some inner insecurity. It was not a stable way to live. Nor did she appear to feel much self worth: at one point she remarked, 'I'm ugly, I don't give a shit.' Of course, Amy was far from ugly – some male interviewers had commented on the striking effect she had on men – but at some fundamental stage her self-worth had clearly been damaged. It does not take a psychiatrist to see that this might point to the problems in the future: the dramatic weight loss, the numerous tattoos that many people believe defaced her and, of course, her heroin addiction. Amy was utterly deserving of the success she was having, but for all the bravado, something was wrong, and it would not be long before her demons came to the surface.

Underneath it all, Amy remained a traditional girl. 'I would like to get married, maybe, but I don't know any men that would be able to handle me 'cos I'm a bit mad,' she said. 'I'm not mad like psychotic mad. You won't come home and find all your suits with the arms cut off – I'd rather cut my man's arms off than disrespect his clothes. I'm a good girlfriend. If I wasn't working, I'd have their dinner on the table every night.'

As she grew in stature, though, she appeared to be revising her opinions about the past. Suddenly, Sylvia Young had become an attractive place to go to school. 'I'm always happy to blow up any misconceptions that people have about stage school, 'cos everyone thinks it's really nasty there, but it's not,' she said firmly. 'I went to the Brit School as well and that was shit. But Sylvia Young set me up to be a strong person.'

She was also beginning to think of the future and, more specifically, where her career would go from here. Most British artists want to break the United States and only a handful succeed; but Amy was determined she would have a go, although not for the reasons most stars do. 'It's important for me that people hear my music but I don't care about conquering vast areas of the world,' she said. 'I love America, it's a much more permissive place. Here in England, everyone's a pop star, innit, whereas in America they believe in the term artist. Here it's "how badly can we get you to fuck up in front of the camera?" They're just waiting for things to go wrong here.' And what about the criticisms she had made of her fellow stars? 'Yeah, but I won't be a mass artist, will I?' she said. 'So I don't think I'll ever have to say, "I'm sorry for the things I've said."'

Amy was beginning to realise, however, that sometimes it didn't hurt to be a little less forthcoming. 'You gotta be a diplomat,' she admitted. 'If you've got an auntie who kisses you, smothers your face, you can't be like "I don't like you auntie, you smother me!" There's times when you can't be like that. My management tell me off. Not tell me off, but say, "Go and apologise to these heads of the record company." I'm like "OK, fuck it, cool, let's go." I'll apologise; I don't give a shit. Sorry, sorry, sorry, sorry. It's just a word, innit?'

But old habits die hard, as she proved with an attack on one of the major names in the music business. 'If I could be in charge of anybody, it would be whoever it is that gives Janet [Jackson] her songs and J.Lo her songs,' she began. 'I would switch them over so that J.Lo has to do all the poppy shit and Janet gets all the sexy R&B that she needs to be doing. There's no point having a hundred people working on tunes that someone [J.Lo] can't even sing. My friend is a singer/songwriter who had to do tunes for J.Lo and they told her purposely not to sing too good, 'cos Jennifer can't sing that. They were like "You need to tone it down" and she was like "Oh, you mean really basic." She can't do anything, apparently.'

But she could get away with it, because she was becoming more popular than ever. In May, she won the Ivor Novello award, something that she was clearly delighted about. 'I haven't got no words,' she said afterwards.

'I'm proud of myself. Bobby Womack gave this to me!'

Afterwards, when she'd calmed down a little, she continued to express her delight. 'I feel wicked; I'm very proud of myself,' she said. 'I never thought I was going to get something. I ain't got no words. This is a big deal for me; it's massive. It's a real award. It's like the judges have said well done, you've done your shit, it's honest and people respect you for that. This is not about how well you perform or how many units you've sold because people like Dido have sold much more than me. I thought Kylie would get it. But I wanted Dizzee to get it. That would have made it for me.'

It was a very well deserved award but, rather ominously, Amy highlighted only too accurately what inspired her to write music. Indeed, in the light of her later history, the following is almost tragic. 'I take out my anger and frustration by writing songs and that's really where *Frank* came from,' she said. 'And now I'm having a great time – everything is going really well with the record. I'm doing a lot of gigs and singing is the thing I love doing most. I will have to start writing for a new album at some point, so I think I'm going to have to take time off and live a normal life so that things can happen to me again that aren't all good. Otherwise I'll have nothing to write about on the next album.' Given the next album was to contain one of her most famous songs to date, about refusing to go into rehab, Amy, alas, did indeed find she had a great deal to write about.

Success was not, however, mellowing her. Katie Melua came in for yet another bashing when Amy was asked about her: 'I pride myself on being different,' she said backstage at the BBC Jazz Awards. 'Jazz is all about pushing the boundaries and experimenting. I have never listened to Katie's music but it is all written for her and she is shit. I have been compared to her but I am nothing like her.'

Katie herself was finally goaded into a reply – a very diplomatic one. 'I have never met Amy,' she said a touch wearily. 'I don't know why she would say these things about me. Maybe she knows things about me that I don't. I don't know her album or listen to her music. But her voice is stunning.'

In the event, the whole lot of the young pretenders in the jazz world – not just Amy and Katie, but Jamie Cullum, Norah Jones, and Joss Stone – were all brought down to size: none of them was even nominated for an award. 'Their songs may be riding high in the charts, but the jazz world refuses to accept them,' said a source at the awards. 'It is absurd, but they are seen as too mainstream, young and inexperienced to be taken seriously. They are seen more as pop stars and were only invited to attract publicity for the event.'

Amy and Katie were certainly going to have to learn to get on. The Gangstarr rapper Guru was planning a new album, *Jazzmatazz Volume 4*, and wanted the two of them, along with Jamie Cullum, Lemar, Jamelia, and a host of others, to appear on it. 'Guru's not had an opportunity to work with many jazz musicians since doing the last *Jazzmatazz* album in 2000,' said a source. 'But he's heard a lot of good things about the young jazz scene that's kicking off in the UK and has made contact with a lot of the big names. He's coming over in two months to start recording the album. Guru's a huge fan of both Amy and Katie, and Lemar and Jamie are definitely going to appear.'

But Amy did not appear willing to kiss and make up with her rivals, whatever Guru might have had in mind. 'Yep, Dido, and Katie Melua are both still a load of shit,' she answered, when asked if her opinion of them remained as low as ever. 'They should never go up on stage in my opinion – they call that music?'

It was beginning to grate with some of her fellow artists, who were beginning to think she was just doing it for the publicity. 'She should shush and let her music talk – if she can,' said Beverley Knight. Various female columnists were also beginning to disapprove. There was a general feeling that she was getting above herself, not least because she repeated her remarks about Madonna, a woman who had by now sold one hundred and fifty million records. Simon Fuller was also thought to have had words behind the scenes.

Katie Melua was certainly displaying grace under fire. 'What was all that about?' she said of Amy's critical remarks. 'It's a real shame because I haven't met Amy yet. I don't know if she meant it but we should sit down and talk about it.'

Amy was put in her place again when it came to the prestigious Mercury music prize. She had been nominated along with Belle and Sebastian, Snow Patrol, Jamelia, and Joss Stone, but it was the Scottish art pop band Franz Ferdinand who walked off with the prize.

Perhaps a little bruised by all this, Amy contented herself – for now – with talking about fashion. 'Yeah, my legs and the boobs – they're my things,' she said, before explaining her own style. 'I bought this great fake Vuitton a while ago – pink, metallic, but that makes it sound really gross, doesn't it? Also, I like the fake Chanel stuff.' However, she also had quite upmarket tastes. 'Tom Ford and Marc Jacobs – what he's done at Vuitton is great,' she said. 'And also labels that have a real legacy, like, well, Vuitton again, but also Missoni and Chanel.' She was not shy, however, of naming the names she didn't like: 'Michael Kors and MaxMara – they just look like really bad high street.'

Amazingly, she then started complimenting her peers. On Christina Aguilera and her new and more modest look: 'She's a talented girl, but you couldn't really see it before when she was wearing those chaps with her ninny hanging out.'

And on Madonna, no less: 'I love the way she's so comfortable with her sexuality.'

However, it wasn't all sweetness and light. On Sienna Miller she said, 'She's got nice clothes, but she just looks like a high-street poster girl, like, really ready-made. I don't want to be the prettiest or the sexiest or whatever. I just want to look different and to look like me.'

And anyway, the fans still loved her. She performed at the Miller Strat Pack concert at Wembley Arena, a celebration of the Fender Stratocaster's fiftieth anniversary. Hank Marvin, more typical than Amy of the age range on stage, had a nice take on the evening: 'Thank you for coming here to support a worthy cause,' he said. 'Old men.'

Another appearance was at the launch of the BlackBerry 7100v superphone at London's Sanderson Hotel, where she was more than annoyed when the audience talked through her act. 'Amy said she thought the guests were rude because they kept talking while she was performing,' said a source who was present. 'After her second set, she said she'd never perform again to such an intimate crowd. Someone then knocked a drink onto the stage. 'Bring me a towel right away,' snapped Amy. 'I'm worried I'll break something.'

Having briefly shown a bit of contrition towards her contemporaries, Amy now seemed determined to start making waves again. There were rumours that Kylie Minogue was considering recording a jazz album: it was like a red rag to a bull. 'What is happening?' demanded Amy. 'She's not an artist. She's a pony ... like a little, cute, beautiful, beautiful pony.'

And of Rod Stewart's *Great American Songbook*: 'It absolutely disgusts me. It's a fucking travesty.'

If truth be told, Amy seemed disinclined to play the game. 'I don't say things because I'm bitter,' she said. 'I say things everyone else is thinking but no one else dares to say. All these boys in guitar bands all want to say how shit everyone else is, but they can't because they can be replaced easily.'

As the year drew to a close, Amy continued to tour, learning the basics as she went. The reviews continued to improve and by the year's end, although she still had a way to go, critics were beginning to concede that she was managing to handle her audience. She was still more comfortable in small gigs rather than huge arenas, but her initial nervousness now seemed almost entirely gone.

In January 2005, there was no surprise when Amy was nominated for Best British Female Solo Artist at the Brits, up against Jamelia, Joss Stone, Natasha Bedingfield, and PJ Harvey, although in the end it was Joss Stone who won. It didn't seem to bother her unduly: shortly afterwards she was singing at the pre-Bafta party at London's Wallace Collection.

However, as the year progressed, there were worrying signs as to what was to come. She was spotted clearly drunk on an increasing basis, while her dress sense appeared to be getting worse and worse. There were reports of very public canoodlings with 'mystery men' and some very erratic behaviour.

One evening, she attended the Teenage Cancer Trust party at London's Eve club and announced, 'I don't normally go to celebrity parties, but this one's free booze and I don't get my cash out until tomorrow. I ain't got no money. The record label won't pay me until I come up with the next album and I'm working on the songs.'

'I go to the gym. I used to go for two hours a day at a place on The Strand. It was well posh. I got that for free too because my friend works at a salon a few doors down and they promote each other's businesses. I have to eat junk food all the time. And look at my spots – they're awful.' It was a pretty bizarre way to behave, even for someone who was developing as wayward a reputation as Amy. And as for that two hours a day at the gym – it was an indication of the kind of compulsive behaviour that was to become increasingly evident over the next few years.

At least her love life was looking up. Tyler James was never going to be a serious boyfriend, but James Bourne from Busted, who had dated Amy briefly while they were at the Brit School of Arts, was now back on the scene and things appeared to be going well between them. 'They have always got on really well,' said a friend of both. 'James thinks that Amy is a top girl.'

By now Amy was becoming a regular fixture on the London music scene, either performing at or attending the numerous parties and gigs about town: she was one of those chosen to sing at 'Happy Birthday To Ya', a concert celebrating Stevie Wonder's fifty-fifth birthday at the Jazz Café. She was booked for the second Cornbury Music Festival and appeared at the Bacardi B-Bar party. She was now regularly making appearances in the gossip columns and generating news even without having a go at her fellow celebs.

But her appearance was beginning to change. Amy had had an attractively rounded figure when she started out:

it was becoming much, much slimmer. And tattoos had started to appear all over her body. Rather ominously, in hindsight, a tattoo of a top pocket, with the word, 'Blake's' appeared on her chest. Several years on, it is now obvious that she and James Bourne were not having that serious a relationship after all, but at the time, the identity of this mysterious Blake was known only to Amy's inner circle. It was soon going to become familiar to very many more.

In fact, behind the scenes, Amy was having a very turbulent period in her life. She had cut down on the drugs, but had met up with Blake Fielder-Civil, who was to cause untold trouble in the future. No one knew about it at the time, but the relationship was extremely turbulent. 'It was my local,' said Amy, when asked where they met. 'I spent a lot of time there, playing pool and listening to jukebox music. More significantly, I used to smoke a lot of weed. I suppose if you have an addictive personality, then you go from one poison to the other. He doesn't smoke weed, so I started drinking more and not smoking as much. And because of that, I just enjoyed stuff more. I'd go out and have a drink.'

'The whole weed mentality is very hip-hop, and when I made my first record, all I was listening to was hip-hop and jazz. The weed mentality is very defensive, very much like, "Fuck you – you don't know me." Whereas the drinking mentality is very "Woe is me. Oh, I love you. I'm gonna lie in the road for you. I don't even care if you never even look my way, I'm always gonna love you."'

When it ended, because Blake admitted he'd been seeing Chloe Kerman, daughter of the restaurateur Nicky Kerman, Amy's behaviour spiralled out of control to such an extent that she did, indeed, have a spell in rehab, although she was later to announce that it had been of no help at all.

'First, I stopped smoking weed and I was happy and content,' she said much later. The she met Blake, fell in love, 'for the first time', and they split up. 'I really think if you have problems and you can't sort them out yourself, you're in trouble anyway,' she said. 'I also got sent to food rehab, and that was exactly the same as the alcohol one. I walked in and was like, "I don't need this", and walked straight back out. I had to tell myself: "Amy, you're not the queen of the world and you don't know everything".'

She was spotted, barefoot, clearly in some distress and rake thin, in Hoxton Market, east London, being helped by a man telling her, 'You're going to have to give up drinking.' She turned twenty-two in September 2005, enormously successful, but giving off clear signs that all was not well.

In the background, unpublicised at the time, Amy's

love life was taking a road that would prove to have a massive impact on her life. In later years, she described her domesticity thus: 'Actually, there is something inside me that is a proper little housewife. I love cooking for him [her then boyfriend], even though he's a chef and knows much more about cooking than I do! I constantly want to look after people, but I've only met a couple of men in my life who deserved or appreciated it. My first proper long-term boyfriend Chris (he's the fella that I wrote my first album about) was lovely, but he didn't really appreciate it. It was my second boyfriend, Blake, who kick-started my domestic instinct. I immediately saw he was someone who hadn't been treated right, so I practically put him in my bag and said, "Right, you're coming with me!"'

For now, and for some months ahead, Amy began to adopt a lower profile. There were fewer criticisms of her fellow stars, and she was seen less often in public. She was, of course, working on her enormously successful second album *Back to Black*, but she was also, as became known a couple of years later, beginning to develop the habits that were to cause such dreadful problems in the future. By mid-2006, her famous curves had all but gone: 'She's got legs like a sparrow and her hipbones were jutting out above her shorts,' said someone who saw her tucking into an all-too-rare takeaway curry. 'She looked unwell.'

But she was still working. In August 2006, she appeared with Mark Ronson – with whom she had been collaborating – at Cabaret Voltaire in Edinburgh, to sing a song from her new album, due out in two months' time. However, her weight loss was now so severe that newspaper commentators were picking up on it: she was now routinely compared to the six-stone size-zero girls who were causing such concern.

Amy rose above it. Three years after the release of *Frank*, she announced some live dates in September 2006. And then, in October, *Back to Black* was released. It garnered fantastic reviews, reassuring all who doubted that Amy was a force with which to be reckoned. 'Winehouse's exceptional, Fifties-styled second album,' is how one critic described it. 'An album so graphically honest – and musically stunning – it makes Lily Allen sound like Marie Osmond,' said Garry Mulholland in *The Observer*. But it also gave a very strong hint as to what she had been up to behind the scenes in the song 'Rehab', the album's forthcoming single.

Amy was back, though it was a very different Amy from the one who had burst onto the scene three years ago, flaunting her curves and popping out of her clothes. This Amy was stick thin, covered with tattoos, and rumoured not only to be overdoing it at the gym (and in many other areas of her life), but to have developed an eating disorder as well. Even Amy realised something was up, although she down played it as much as she could. 'I think people just want to say things for the sake of saying things,' she said. 'I'm not dusting it off like, "I don't have a problem". I obviously do have a problem, but it's not as out of control as it has been. I wouldn't be able to discuss it if it wasn't in my pocket and controllable.'

Amy had been lying low for the previous two years, but the release of *Back to Black* heralded a whole new phase in her life, one that was going to be a constant from that moment on. Previously, people had been interested in Amy because of her music and her propensity to badmouth her fellow artists. From this moment onwards, they were interested in her because of her music and her life.

Whether she realised it or not, Amy had made the transition from being just another singer – albeit it an excellent one – to a subject of absolute fascination because of her all-too-obvious problems. A new jazz diva on the scene is one thing, but a new jazz diva who lives her life like a high-octane soap opera is quite another. Men, booze, drugs, an eating disorder – all were to play an increasingly large role in Amy's life from now on, while Amy herself, ironically, was finally driven into rehab. The time was to come when she would stop saying, 'No, no, no'.

That, however, was still some way off. Amy was showing herself to be as tough as ever: she held a low-key birthday party in a north London pub, only for it to be overrun with gate crashers. She took matters in hand herself. 'Amy wanted to keep things very low key, so only invited a handful of her closest friends,' said a friend who was present. 'But the venue leaked out, so lots of undesirables stopped by. Foolishly they didn't count on her defending her privacy like a prizefighter. She wasn't chuffed and nearly decapitated one bloke when she lobbed a candlestick at him.'

Amy was beginning to analyse where she had got to in her life and how her work was progressing. 'I'm only twenty-three, so I don't feel I'm experienced with men, or with people in general,' she said in *The Observer*. 'All the songs I write are about human dynamics, whether it's with girlfriends, boyfriends, or family. When I did the last album, *Frank*, I was a very defensive, insecure person, so when I sang about men it was all like, "Fuck you. Who do you think you are?" The new album is more, "I will fight for you. I would do anything for you", or "It's such a shame we couldn't make it work". I feel like I'm not so teenage about relationships.'

By this time Amy had split up with Blake and was ensconced with a new man, Alex. She seemed content with her life. 'I've never been a boyfriend kind of girl,' she said.

'I'm too selfish. A couple of years ago I would have said that I would end up as one of those women who lives with twenty cats and forty piles of newspapers, but I'm thinking a bit more optimistically now because I've met someone I really like. I've been with Alex for six months and he moved in about a month after we met – it felt natural, and not at all scary. He's like my best mate, which probably sounds really sad.'

It didn't, and many wished that Amy had stayed with Alex, rather than linking up again with Blake. But she would not live her life according to what other people wanted, and was also very irritated by the people who kept harping on about her dramatic weight loss. 'The papers go on about how I lost weight, but I didn't even notice myself losing it,' she said. 'I used to smoke £200 worth of weed a week – that's two ounces – which is disgusting, and it made me eat crap food on impulse. I lost the weight when I stopped smoking weed and got into the gym instead. I like my gym because there are all these sweaty men around to gear me up and get my adrenaline going. You want to sweat and look good.'

But was she taking it too far? Amy was about to start on a roller coaster, one that would certainly take her to the brink. It was going to be a bumpy ride.

They Tried To Put Me Into Rehab ...

AMY HAD BEEN attracting attention from the moment she hit the music scene, but from this moment onward, just about everything she did made the pages. And, it must be said, she did not help herself. One of her first promotional appearances for the new album was when she went on the Charlotte Church Show: it was a shambles from start to finish and the reason was all too obvious. She was slurring into the microphone, and it went downhill from there.

'Amy was having real trouble reading the autocue and it soon became clear that something was seriously up,' said a source in the studio. 'It was a bit of a car-crash moment. She was also shoving her head into camera shots with other guests and didn't seem to have a clue what was going on.'

Nor was that all. She smashed her foot into a glass table as she stood up, and embarrassed her fellow guest Keith Allen, not exactly a stranger to boisterous behaviour himself. 'He looked a little thrown by the situation and didn't know where to look,' said the source. 'Even by his standards, it was clear she was more than a little merry.'

Worse was to come for the show's finale. 'The plan was to do Michael Jackson's "Beat It", but Amy kept forgetting the words,' said the source. 'In the end, they had to do three takes. Charlotte was a real pro but even her patience was wearing thin.'

Amy, however, was at a stage where she was point blank denying she had a problem. She was open about the fact that she'd been diagnosed with manic depression: 'I told the fella in charge that drinking is symptomatic of my depression,' she said. 'I'm not an alcoholic.'

Even so, she was still holding it together enough to set out on a new tour. She was getting better and better at live singing, and one reviewer pointed out that while she still looked like a gawky teenager, she sounded like a forty-year-old black woman from Brooklyn. The power of her voice was unmistakeable.

Unfortunately, the drinking was getting increasingly worrying. Amy admitted to an experience in the Proud Gallery, in Camden, north London, in which she hit another woman: 'This girl came up to me and said I was brilliant,' she related. 'Two seconds later she turned around to my boyfriend, pointed at me and said, "She's fucked up". So I punched her right in the face – which she wasn't expecting, because girls don't do that. My bloke Alex took me outside to calm me down and I kneed him in the balls then punched him in his face, too. When I've been on the booze recently, it's turned me into a really nasty drunk.' That was for sure, and although Amy seemed torn between self-congratulation and slight regret, it wasn't anything to boast about. It heralded trouble ahead.

Amy was certainly nothing if not honest. 'I have had problems with my weight,' she said in an interview with the *Daily Star*. 'Everyone was going on about it being caused by cocaine, but it wasn't a drugs thing. I was somewhere between being bulimic and anorexic, and I wasn't well. The thing is, you'd be surprised how many girls have had eating problems at some point in their lives; splitting up with my last boyfriend was what triggered mine. I was doing a few drugs, but only dabbling. Cocaine isn't really my thing and I was never really on it.' The boyfriend in question was Blake.

But for now she seemed besotted with Alex. 'My new album, *Back To Black*, is definitely inspired in part by my man,' she continued. 'His name's Alex and we met playing pool in this pub six months ago. We're both very passionate and I know he would die for me. He's helped me put the weight back on – he's a chef. But I still do the cooking at home, because I believe in being a good woman to my man.'

There was a new girl on the scene by this time: Lily Allen. Did Amy feel like passing on a few words? 'I love her, but I wouldn't try to give her advice, because she'd probably tell me to fuck off,' said Amy, who had clearly now learnt some tact. 'I've met her and she'll do well in America, too, because they'll love her accent. All I will say is that if you slag people off, it says a lot more about you yourself and you can look a right dick.'

But she was cheerfully thinking of the future – and being as frank as ever. 'I want to get a load of celebrity boys in my next video,' she said. 'I'd like Serge from Kasabian, but we had a little thing together and he's been funny with me ever since. He's still beautiful, though. My mate Rhys Ifans would do it. Once, I fell asleep in his fireplace. I'd been strutting around his house half-naked and then I just passed out there because it was cosy. He loves me because I always shout at him. Boys love it when I shout at them.'

And above all, of course, there was still the music. 'I still feel like a black girl trapped in a white girl's body, but I no longer feel the need to try to make my voice do difficult jazz stuff,' Amy said. 'This album is everything I wanted it to be. I think the British music scene is finally getting there. Ears have been opened by the Zutons and the Libertines, and Pete Doherty's a genius and a poet, even if Babyshambles are basically shit. I wouldn't put Kasabian in there, though. All their backing vocals are the same and Serge has no fresh ideas. They are lovely boys, though.' There's nothing like damning with faint praise.

Until now, Amy's public excesses – the drink, the drugs – had fitted in well with her slightly louche persona. The singers of torch songs, after all, tended to have some instability in their own lives (it added poignancy to the music and, given that Amy wrote her own songs, gave her the subject matter for her lyrics. It also added a depth to her vocals), even Frank Sinatra didn't reach the prime of his own vocal powers until, via his relationship with his second wife, Ava Gardner, he had known the intensity of suffering through having loved and lost. But now concerns began to arise that Amy was going a little too far. It's one thing to have a slightly wild side to your life, but quite another to show, in your very early twenties, such signs of self-destruction, and that was what Amy was beginning to do now. She was taking it too far, becoming too excessive.

Her record bosses began to express real concern. The appearance on Charlotte Church's show had alerted them to quite the extent Amy was overdoing it: indeed, some reports said that she'd had champagne for breakfast; vodka, whisky, Baileys, and liqueurs at lunch; and more at the Green Room before the show. The wonder was not that she'd performed so badly, but that she'd been able to perform at all.

'Amy is a vibrant character and the record company love the fact that she's got spirit, but her consumption of alcohol is seriously getting out of hand,' said a source at Island Records. 'She's turning up to interviews out of her head and she usually sinks more booze while being grilled about her life. We're all worried that she's going off the rails. She's been told that if she doesn't curb things, she will have to go into rehab to sort herself out. She's managed to resist going in the past, but things have never been this bad.'

Ironically, her single 'Rehab', was going from strength to strength. If the critics were still a little cautious about Amy's live performances, no such reservations were voiced about her new record. Both the single and the album were receiving wildly enthusiastic praise from all sides, with a real awareness of a sensational talent in the music industry's midst.

One of her fans in the music industry was the 'Modfather' Paul Weller, who was putting together a selection of young talent for the Electric Proms. They included the Dirty Pretty Things' Carl Barat, Rich Archer from Hard-Fi, and, of course, Amy. 'Paul keeps a very close eye on what's going on in the charts and is always keen to support young talent,' said a source. 'He was a big fan of The Libertines and loves Dirty Pretty Things, so he asked Carl to appear. Amy Winehouse's feistiness has always attracted him and Hard-Fi are personal faves. He likes them so much he joined the lads on stage when they played Brixton Academy early this year.' The show received sensational reviews.

Amy herself remained defiant about her bad habits. Given the name of her latest single, the subject of rehab reared its head constantly. Amy was unrepentant about her decision not to go, saying that it would be of no help. 'Rehab is like Butlins – it's a holiday camp,' she said. 'It's an everyday thing for some people – like going to Tesco. I was having a particularly nasty time with things and just drinking and drinking. My management said they were taking me to rehab.

I asked my dad if he thought I needed to go. He said no, but that I should give it a try. So I did, for just fifteen minutes. I went in said "hello" and explained that I drink because I am in love and have fucked up the relationship. Then I walked out. I don't need help because if I can't help myself I can't be helped.'

That relationship was, of course, with Blake, and it appeared he had been the inspiration for much of *Back to Black*, too. 'My songs are very honest about a relationship that didn't survive,' said Amy, who became increasingly forthcoming as she went on. 'I only write songs when there is a problem that I can't get through myself. I write a song about it to put myself past it. *Back To Black* is when you've finished a relationship and you go back to what's comfortable for you. My ex went back to his girlfriend and I went back to drinking and dark times. 'Tears Dry On Their Own' is a track about the break-up with Blake, my ex. Most of these songs are about him. I shouldn't have been in a relationship with him because he was already involved with someone else – a bit too close to home. The song is about when we split up and saying to myself: "Yes, you're sad but you'll get over it." And I did.'

'I still talk to Blake and, once we got over the initial pain, it was fine. I believe you can be mates with your ex. I'm such a single girl and when I'm with someone I'm totally with them and I want to be friends for ever, whether we're having sex or not. Sex is just a base level thing. It's not important. I'm still really close to him as a friend and nothing more – though Alex, my boyfriend now, doesn't like me seeing him which is understandable, I guess.'

In actual fact, Amy was anything but over him, as subsequent events were to make clear. But she was putting on a brave face, and resolutely talking about her music and how it was developing. 'I'm not a jazz girl any more,' she said. 'I've gone off it. I can't even listen to *Frank* any more

68

– in fact, I've never been able to. I like playing the tracks live because that's different but listening to them is another story. Even when I was at record signings and the store would be playing *Frank* in the background, I'd be begging them to play something else!'

'These songs are more accessible than the tracks on *Frank*, as jazz is quite elitist. People didn't get it. I've been listening to Sixties bands and girl groups and it came out in the writing on *Back to Black*; stuff like the Shangri-Las and The Velvet Underground. There are a lot of bands that are Sixties influenced at the moment, but I guess I'm the only girl doing it.'

Under the circumstances, it was perhaps no surprise that Amy's relationship with Alex appeared to be under some strain. The pair were pictured having a huge and very public row in a pub in Camden: 'Amy was telling him in no uncertain terms what she thought of him,' said a witness to the argument. 'He tried to reason with her on the stairs but then he thought better of it and stormed off. Amy looked really upset and although her friends tried to cheer her up, she was having none of it.' Or, to put it another way, she was still not over Blake.

There had been other changes behind the scenes which, in hindsight, possibly had a bad effect on Amy, allowing her to run yet further out of control. She might have resented the controlling hand of Simon Fuller but he did see the dangers in the way she was behaving and tried to calm her down. However, Amy had by now changed management and was running wilder than ever.

'It was my old management's idea to stick me in rehab but I'm not with them anymore and there's not much cause for me to go to rehab now,' she said. 'When it was suggested to me, I went to see the guy at the centre for ten minutes just so I could say to the record company that I went. I literally walked in and walked out. I knew it wasn't for me. I knew I'd end up sitting in a room with fifteen depressing people. I thought, forget this. Is there a piano in here or what? I'd rather be playing the guitar somewhere. Music will always be my outlet.'

However, Amy was clearly in denial. Far from having sorted her problems out, she was point blank denying she had any in the first place. 'I don't need drugs or alcohol,' she said. 'That's not a dependency. It's something to do when I'm bored. But I was definitely drinking too much. I've always had a high tolerance for alcohol. The kind of states I was getting myself into was a joke. I'll admit it was a joke. My friends would find me at six o'clock on a Saturday night, already drunk. I shouldn't have been drunk at that time. I'd be wrecked from the day before, having stayed up all night and I'd still be up. Or I'd have passed out at five o'clock. It wasn't very healthy.'

And behind it all was Blake. Amy couldn't stop talking about him: she was clearly as besotted as ever, another worrying development with the benefit of hindsight. 'I was really depressed,' she said in yet another interview. 'I was in love with someone and it fell through. A lot of it was to do with bad choices and misgivings. We were both to blame for the split. Now I take it one day at a time. I really do try not to drink, but I'm the kind of person that if I place too much importance on it, then I will slip up and disappoint myself. I'm a very self-destructive person.'

As for the fiasco on the Charlotte Church show, Amy was remarkably impenitent. 'I don't think I was out of control but I was drunk and I was being really stupid,' she said. 'I do embarrass myself a lot. But I don't regret anything. I'm me. I was drunk and I'm often drunk. But the thing about Charlotte Church's show is that she goes on like it's such a big knees up and everyone's having a laugh. So I did have a laugh and they didn't like that. She asked me onto the show, so she must know I'm a bit of a liability. But she's not my mate, so I don't know how she was like afterwards. She was probably angry that she couldn't have a drink as well.'

It was an admirable way to shrug it off. And indeed,

Amy had even managed to gain a little weight, appearing slightly less emaciated than she had done before. 'I did have problems with food at some stage,' she said straight-forwardly. 'I just didn't eat and I was exercising a lot. I don't mind speaking about it because it's something so many young girls do. It is not a disease. It's so much more common than that. I feel so lucky now. I have put on three quarters of a stone since I was at my skinniest and I'm really happy with my weight. I've definitely got my curves back. I've got my boobs and my bum back and I feel great. There did come a point when I told myself I had to put on weight. It was horrible. My best friend saw me and was trying not to cry. She didn't want to upset me but I saw that it was affecting her. Friends tried to talk me round. But that's what your friends do because they love you, they look after you.'

Work had also taken its toll. 'Because I was working so hard on the album, any thought of eating well and being healthy took a back seat,' said Amy. 'Making the album was all I cared about. I was so focused on it.'

Amy also now revealed her favourite cocktail was Rickstasy: three parts vodka, one part Southern Comfort, one part banana liqueur, and one part Baileys. 'By the time you've had two of them you don't even try to go any-where,' said Amy happily. 'Sit down and stay down, until the birds start singing. I'm not a sick drunk. I'm a violent drunk.'

She wasn't joking. She punched a man in a pub for irritating behaviour: he was, 'punctuating his stories by slapping his hand on our table. It was just really really unfunny. I have a really good time some nights, but then I push it over the edge and ruin my boyfriend's night. I'm an ugly dickhead drunk, I really am.'

It was also becoming increasingly clear that Amy really did have a problem with food. Not only did she not always eat well, but she had started exercising far too much, another giveaway of an anorexic. But she continued to be open about this, too. 'I had a period where I struggled a little bit with eating disorders,' she said to one interviewer. 'Very, very recently. It was only a year ... only a few ... I only really stopped it ... The thing is, if you're an addict, you don't get over it, you're just in remission. So I won't sit here and go, "Yeah, I don't have a problem with food any more". I do forget to eat a lot, and I do have my odd days where I think, "You can't eat because you ate that yesterday". But I think all modern girls are like that and I don't like to make too big a thing about it. I'm attached to the gym but that's not a vice, that's a good thing.'

But was it? It was becoming excessive, just as her drug taking had been, and she even talked about it in the same terms. 'Going to the gym is the best drug,' she said. 'I go four times a week. It gives me the buzz I need. I didn't even notice myself losing the weight. When I was a teenager, I struggled with eating. I wasn't anorexic or bulimic, but I was suffering. I pulled myself out of it and I'm not like that now. It's something I've got over. Some people reckoned I looked healthier when I was bigger, but I had terrible skin and no energy. I've recently put on seven pounds.'

But drinking still remained a very big part of her life. 'It's too much of a drinking culture, everything tastes better with a drink,' she said. 'Like, watch TV: glass of wine. Cooking dinner: glass of champagne.' As for rehab, the more she talked about it, the more it was obvious that it really hadn't worked. When she went in, she was told her drinking was, '"symptomatic of the depression". I said "That's correct." And the man said: "Well, I'm an alcoholic and I've been this way for fifty years" – which is tragic isn't it? Horrible. I don't ever want to be one of those people who can't be around drink. And I'm not the kind of person who sees someone do a shot and goes, "I can do that! I can do three!" I'm not like that. I can drink a lot and have a good time and not be absolutely twatted though. So yeah, he asked me to fill in this form. It was a psychological thing – how much do you drink, that kind of thing – and

I said, how long's it gonna take? He said half an hour, so I said no.'

Her talent allowed her to get away with it. She appeared on *Late With ... Jools Holland*, and this time her appearance was a great success. There was talk of her contributing to the soundtrack of a future James Bond movie. Mark Ronson, the producer of *Back to Black*, was fulsome in his praise of her. 'One of the funniest things about having "hit" songs is hearing something everywhere that came about because you had an idea for a piano line at 3am, or, as with Robbie Williams's "Lovelight", making a beat on a $2,000 drum machine and then you see a video on MTV that cost more than your entire apartment,' he once said. 'Amazing. For me, the ultimate thing is to work with a great band and singer without having to alter it digitally. With someone like Amy Winehouse, you can tell it's the real deal.'

Interviewers also loved her. Although she could be tricky, she was also extremely mischievous, something that went down very well with the people she met. At a photoshoot at her old school, Amy deliberately set off the fire alarm and couldn't stop laughing about it afterwards. 'It was so cool,' she said. 'The headmistress hated me when I was little and she hated me today. She knew it was me; it was great.'

Actually, to be totally accurate, it was her friend, as Amy later confessed. But it was clear she had relished every second of it. 'I was going to a photoshoot at the school,' she recalled a few months later. 'One of my old teachers was there – this cold-blooded bitch; she bleeds ice. She's had the same haircut since 1840. I was there with my friend and after the shoot we were like, "Miss, hello Miss, can we have a look round the school?" and she was like, grudgingly, "Okay" and we went to the art room and my friend wandered off. Next thing, he shouted, "Run! I've smashed the fire alarm!" and the whole school was evacuated. It was the highlight of my life. I was saying, "I do hope it's just a drill, Miss" – and her face was a picture.'

Interviewers also adored her openness. 'I've got nothing to hide,' she said. 'I'm just a young girl who gets fucked up sometimes. Sometimes my head is screwed on tighter than bolts, but a lot of the time I do mess up and lose the plot like everyone does. But because I'm so defensive and sensitive I lash out a lot. I'm not a nice drunk. I get defensive about it because it's a problem. If it wasn't, I'd be like "yep I'm a pisshead". But it's not the bane of my life and I'm not at the point now where I wake up and go, "Where's that bottle of Jack Daniel's?" I was like that. But I know I set myself right up calling my song "Rehab".'

She was still, however, able to focus on the music. *Back*

to Black had a more R'n'B sound to it than *Frank*, and it had come about much more quickly as well. It took her four years to write *Frank*, but her second album spilled out in six months. She was also much more positive about mainstream pop than she had been previously, acknowledging its influence on the music she was making now.

'I love that dramatic Sixties girl group stuff,' she said of *Back to Black*, which by now had been called the best British soul album since Soul II Soul's *Club Classics, Volume 1*. 'It's all sound effects and atmosphere and you can almost hear their hairstyles. It's an era I definitely should have been born in.'

Amy also came across as oddly romantic, having dedicated the album to 'anyone who falls in love every day'. Amy hastily denied that. 'I meant falling in love with the day itself, not with people,' she said. 'You know what I saw the other day? This little old tramp polishing his boots and I thought, "Go on, son!" That kind of thing just swells my heart. I just like people who are warm and lovely and who see the nice things in people rather than seeing the world as shit.'

In the wake of the release of *Back to Black*, however, Amy's own love life seemed to be taking a turn for the worse. It was quite clear to those in the know that she was still in love with Blake, and this was beginning to rub off on her relationship with Alex. They had recently had a row, she revealed, and this time it looked as if they may not make it up.

'Usually he throws a fit and I follow him down the road, but this time I said, "You should probably just go",' said Amy, with her characteristic honesty. 'We're at a point where our relationship has become very domesticated and there's no romance anymore, no fireworks. But I'll make it work with him because I love him so much.' She probably thought she did, too – but Blake's name had already been tattooed on her chest and it was soon to become clear that his mark on her was permanent in other ways as well.

She was, quite understandably, enjoying her success. 'My attitude has changed,' she told one interviewer. 'I never used to believe that I'd get anywhere and thought people wouldn't like me. When I made *Frank* it was a learning curve for me and for the record company, because I'm such a fruit loop. I never really wanted it, you know? I was like, "Are you sure you want to pay for me to make an album? Are you really sure?" I was insecure. But now I'm a lot more inclined to think that the world is yours if you want to take it.'

It was an admirable sentiment, but one that Amy was going to struggle to live up to. She might have kicked drugs for now and replaced them with the gym, but her weight was still dangerously low and she still carried the demons that caused all the problems in the first place. She had established herself as a major talent but, alas, was also showing signs that so many great talents do: self-destructiveness. And while her drug use had been excessive in the past, it was about to spiral totally out of control. Amy was a woman with a great future in front of her – but she badly needed to keep herself under control.

You Know I'm
No Good

THE RELEASE of *Back to Black* and the subsequent tour in its wake reminded everyone that, for all her outrageous behaviour, it was Amy's talent and music that had put her in the spotlight in the first place. Her stage performances were coming on well, and what one critic described as her 'larger than life' personality was coming through: 'We'll get the old ones out of the way first,' was one typical introduction to some numbers during a concert, as she waved to her mother on the balcony. Her next single, 'You Know I'm No Good' was going to be released in the New Year: professionally, she was on a roll.

More acclaim came when she made the *NME* Cool List, one of a number of women that year to do so. 'This year's Cool List is a testament to the raft of hugely talented women who have taken hold of the music scene in 2006,' said Conor McNicholas, the editor of *NME*. 'From Beth to Lily to Karen, they've brought new energy to a scene dominated by men. They're also living proof that you can still rock a crowd when you're wearing stilettos.' Whether

Amy, who came in at number fifty, was equally pleased was a matter of conjecture. 'Why am I in the cool list?' she inquired. 'I'm a dickhead.'

Amy certainly had fans in the industry. Liam Gallagher was singing her praise loudly: 'Liam was a really lovely guy – he was very down to earth and seems to know how lucky Oasis are being able to do what they do,' said Tom Dunne of Today FM, who met him when Oasis visited Dublin. 'And he only rated three acts from this year – Kasabian, Amy Winehouse, and his missus Nicole Appleton's All Saints. He gave All Saints a few shameless plugs – but he would get into serious trouble for slagging off his wife's album. He added he hadn't been writing any songs lately as all his guitar strings are broken.'

The new album continued to be played with the kind of rapturous reviews that Amy was getting used to: behind the scenes, though, she was no closer to calming down. Asked if she was cutting back on her twenty-unit-a-day drinking habit, she confided, 'No. It's been that way for a year. It is what it is. I'll stop at some point. When? I don't know.' She then added, 'I now have a lovely boyfriend. Apart from my dog running away, I'm happy.' That lovely boyfriend was Alex, with whom she seemed to have reconciled.

But her mood swings were now beginning to influence her behaviour, whatever situation she found herself in. A visit to her old school – the Brit School in Surrey – turned into a fiasco because of a squabble with Alex, resulting in Amy storming out in tears and refusing to take part in the scheduled filming of the visit, to be broadcast in *The Brits Are Coming*. 'It was chaos,' said a source present at the time. 'Some of the younger children were crying because they were so looking forward to seeing Amy perform. And the production staff just looked at each in disbelief, not knowing what too say. We tried to get her to change her mind, but she was having none of it and kept shouting "no".'

The pupils felt the same way. 'We wish Katie [Melua] had come instead for the filming because we wouldn't have got any diva-like behaviour from her,' said one. 'Amy was in such a state and just crying. She is an idol to many of us here because of what she's achieved so soon after leaving, and we couldn't believe how she behaved.'

But her peers in the industry continued to adore her. 'How did a twenty-three-year-old from North London end up sounding like someone who once accompanied Billie Holiday to the off licence?' one critic inquired. Others were swooning over the new single. Her professional standing couldn't have been higher. But she was still not averse to picking a fight, and one rather public spat came with the seventeen-year-old Peaches Geldof, who was hosting the

AOL Music Live! event at Kentish Town Forum in north London. It came when both decided they needed to use the loo.

'Amy must have been desperate to use the toilet as she marched straight into the grubby area to find the cubicles full,' said a witness to the row. 'So she knocked on one door and kept knocking and knocking. Peaches had only been in there a second, but Winehouse was determined to use the loo. She started banging her fists on the door and yelling: "Come on, I need to go – now!" and at one stage literally went to kick the door. Clearly by this point, a startled Peaches had had enough and quickly opened the door to find Winehouse glaring at her. Peaches stuck up for herself and told Winehouse she shouldn't be so rude, but Winehouse wasn't having any of it. And she pushed past Peaches into the loo muttering the word "brat".'

Amy was all together more sympathetic to Peaches later in the night, however. Peaches was actually booed off the stage, eliciting words of comfort from Amy later on. 'I really like Peaches and I think she's a nice girl, so I felt bad for her when the crowd responded like that,' she said.

Amy herself was called to step into the breach, and couldn't help but let her customary mouthiness take hold, with a dig at Keisha Buchanan. 'I did an AOL music gig in my manor, Camden,' she related. 'Peaches Geldof was presenting and when I came off stage my manager said to me: "Peaches has left and there's no one to introduce the Sugababes." I said I'd do it. I love The Sugababes, but Keisha's a bit ... well, let's just say she needs to pull the pickle out of her arse.'

Amy's wild side was too much in evidence, so it was perhaps inevitable that there were plans to link up with possibly the only man in the music business who could give Amy a run for her money: Pete Doherty. The two were keen to do some work together, as Amy revealed: 'Pete wanted to do a Billie Holiday cover and I was like, "No, let's write something together",' she said. 'I like writing songs. He's an amazing songwriter and I'd love to be able to say that I wrote a song with Pete Doherty.'

The feeling was, apparently, mutual. 'Pete and Amy have formed a bit of a mutual appreciation society,' said a source close to both of them. 'It's early stages and they're still hammering out on what label the new material will come out. But, time permitting, they'll be in the studio early next year.'

They certainly had other interests in common, too. Amy was drinking as much as ever and it showed: one embarrassing incident at a restaurant was witnessed at London's Cottons restaurant. 'It was 7pm but she was totally out of it,' said one diner who was present. 'She went to the loo and when she came back her trousers weren't done up properly, you could see her bottom. Then she was walking to the bar and fell flat on her face. In the end a member of staff carried her out, but she forgot to pay her bill.' It was, apparently, settled the following day.

As Christmas loomed, Amy flew to New York to work on Mark Ronson's new album. She took the opportunity to fit in a romantic break with Alex as well. 'It's funny how these stories about us rowing in pubs and having a hard time go flying around, and I'm here lying in bed with him in New York – all loved up,' she told one journalist. 'People love concentrating on the negatives, and we are a fiery couple so it is easy for them. But I love him and we've worked through our bad patch to be happy for Christmas.'

As for Mark: 'Me and him just click. He asked me to record with him for his own album so there was no way I'd turn him down. Music is in my blood and if I ever lost my voice, I don't know what I'd do.'

Her work might have been important to her, but in other areas of her life, she continued to careen out of control. Her weight was still plummetting, and her drinking was getting worse. Still, however, she was adamant that the subject matter of her most famous song was not for her. 'Rehab works for some people but for some it doesn't,' she said. 'I've got a few mates who are in and out all the time.

But I'm of the school of thought that if you can't sort something out for yourself, no one can help you. You're lost if you can't sort yourself out. I do think drinking long-term is a lot worse than doing heroin or something – alcohol's a real poison. But at certain times I think: "I have got to have a drink, I can't get through this." The other day was the first day in ages I didn't have a drink, and the next day I was like a little baby squirrel, all bright-eyed and bushy-tailed.'

'[But] I went to this restaurant and my boyfriend was like: "Do you remember what happened last time we were here? Me and that head waiter had to carry you out of here and you were trying to punch and kick us at the same time." I was like: "Oh, my God!" So when we left I wrote a message on the bill saying: "Sorry for the drama, here's a massive tip." Sometimes my management tells me off for drinking. But the other day after Alex and I had one of our splits, I had to go to work and I asked my manager's assistant to get me some mini-bottles of Jack Daniels. I told her: "Listen, if you want to have a nice day, please get me some alcohol, then I'll be sweet as a nut."'

Amy's strange dichotomy between the wild and the domestic continued. One minute she was confessing to the excesses of alcohol; the next she was coming across as a mother figure – albeit it to a pretty wild crowd. 'A lot of my mates are drug addicts,' she said. 'If I see them in a bad way, I'm like, "Come back to mine and I'll make you a shepherd's pie."' There was no doubt that she did so, as well. Friends frequently spoke about her hospitality, and the need to make sure that everyone was fed.

But she remained as outspoken as ever. She might have made her reputation as a jazz diva, but she certainly wasn't going to confine herself to jazz clubs, in which she could have no fun. 'You go to a hip-hop club and everybody's smoking weed, having fun,' she said. 'Go to a jazz club and you can't do anything, because some fifty-year-old bloke is on stage with a saxophone.' Nor had her opinions of her fellow artists softened. 'Jamie Cullum?' she said in an interview. 'Nah, lift music.' And on another occasion, when she was asked if she'd like to duet with Katie Melua (admittedly, a red rag to a bull), she said, 'I'd rather have cat AIDS.'

Now that Amy was practically establishment, she spent New Year's Eve where the establishment does – Jools Holland's annual *Hootenanny* on BBC2. She also made another end-of-year line-up, this one slightly less welcome: the now notorious performance of 'Beat It' was pronounced by the TV critic Garry Bushell as the worst performance of the year (with some justification). 'She made Pete Doherty at Live 8 seem almost coherent', he wrote.

Nor was her appearance on *Hootenanny* an unqualified

success. Onlookers were shocked at how thin she'd become and, as was becoming habitual, she was clearly rather the worse for wear. 'There were all these great stars at *Hootenanny* and she was the only one who couldn't do it in one take,' tutted an insider on the show. 'Her boobs kept falling out of her clothes. She had got really drunk, even though it was recorded a couple of weeks before it went on air.' This kind of behaviour was going beyond the norms of rock 'n' roll – it was quite clearly going to take its toll.

At the start of 2007, a year that was to prove her most momentous – and troubled – *Back to Black* was nominated for a South Bank Show Award. Meanwhile, 'You Know I'm No Good' had been released, prompting the usual ecstatic critical reaction, with one reviewer remarking how impressive it was to be so jaded at just twenty-four.

A quick break in Miami with Alex was followed by a gig at the London nightclub G-A-Y. Amy was unable to perform for long: she and Kelly Osbourne had spent the day on the lash, and it was beginning to show. 'Amy managed one song quite well – then legged it,' said an onlooker. 'The organiser came out and said Amy was throwing up and to bear with her. But she never came back. Everyone was booing.'

Another onlooker put it rather more bluntly. 'She was clearly out of her brains and was trying not to be sick during her one song,' he said. 'It was awful. The club owner Jeremy Joseph tried to tell the crowd she had food poisoning, but they were having none of it. They could see for themselves she was the worse for wear from drink. She looked like she was going to cry. She had been on a bender with Kelly Osbourne. It looks like a spell in rehab is in order.' Amy herself was livid at suggestions that Kelly was leading her astray. 'Kelly is like my conscience telling me when I've had enough,' she said. 'Without her I'd probably be dead.'

Of course, Amy was well known for overdoing it, but there were hints that something a little more troublesome was going on. She, incidentally, maintained that she was jetlagged and had a virus, when interviewed by Jo Whiley on Radio 1, who also took the opportunity to ask Amy what she kept in her enormous beehive of a hairstyle. 'Phone, some loose change, and some action figures,' Amy replied.

But she was also enjoying playing up to her image. 'I asked a friend of mine why men never chat me up and he said it's because they are terrified of me,' she recounted rather gleefully. 'I suppose it's the Russell Brand hair, the tattoos, the fact I like playing pool, and swearing like a bloke. There are too many meek people in this world. I'm not one of them!'

While her love life was gaining momentum behind the

scenes, so too was praise for the new album. *Back to Black* had gone to number one in the album charts – a mixed blessing, in some ways, because while it confirmed her as one of the leading talents of the day, it also rather allowed her to continue to get away with increasingly erratic behaviour. Had Amy been forced to cool it at the beginning of 2007, she might not have had so many problems towards the end of the year – but for now, at least, her success gave her license to misbehave.

It was all grist to the mill. Amy was really learning how to play the game now, and as public interest intensified in her outspoken personality, she got very good at doling out tidbits to keep them wanting more. Asked about the most expensive thing she ever bought, she replied, 'My heart back from someone who may or may not have deserved it.' She followed that up by saying that her most treasured possession was her loyalty, her chosen super power would be super sexuality, and her favourite smells were petrol and hairspray. Oh, and that love feels like, 'a disease that consumes you eternally.' Amy was quite clearly born to be a star.

When the Brit nominations were announced in January 2007, it was no surprise that Amy was on the list for Best British Female, up against newcomer Lily Allen (who in terms of attitude and exposure was giving even Amy a run for her money), Corinne Bailey Rae, Jamelia, and Nerina Pallot. She was also up for the Mastercard British Album Award, against Arctic Monkeys, Lily Allen (again), Muse, and Snow Patrol. In addition, Amy was going to perform at the awards ceremony. *Back to Black* was still hovering around the top of the charts, occasionally slipping to two and then bouncing back up to the top slot again; praise continued to flood her way.

For all singers, however, the biggest prize is to conquer the United States. Most don't: even Robbie Williams has never managed to get a toehold in the land of the free. Although it was a small-scale gig, it was thus nonetheless a big moment when Amy held her first concert in the States at Joe's Pub in New York, and, despite having a few drinks before hand, absolutely wowed the audience. The Americans were as taken aback as the Brits that the source of that voice was a young white woman, rather than a middle-aged black one, while members of the crowd included Jay-Z and Mos Def. It was a triumphant introduction to the other side of the pond – although there was still, as she would be well aware, a very long way to go.

Amy was by now an acknowledged style icon. She was regularly cited as one of the wave of beautiful new 'indie chicks' to be spotted about town and with her beehive hair, trademark black eyeliner and scarlet lipstick, she was certainly a striking woman. There were even articles in newspapers and magazines about how to achieve the look – pale foundation and black hair dye featured largely.

Slightly less fortunate was her growing collection of tattoos. While it is now commonplace for women to have tattoos, Amy was covering herself in them. She had an explanation: 'I like looking at pretty pictures. I get bored looking in the mirror and seeing the same thing. So I just keep getting more and more.' But it could also be taken as a sign of self-mutilation. That Amy had demons was plain enough to see, and distorting a very attractive appearance was clearly one way in which it manifested itself.

But while Amy was so clearly at the top of her game, no one seemed inclined to worry. *Back to Black* remained at the top of the album charts, while in January 2007 she won a prize at the South Bank Show Awards for Best Pop Album. She used the occasion, as was her wont, to say something memorable: in this case she spoke about the racist bullying of the Indian actress Shilpa Shetty in *Celebrity Big Brother*. Surprisingly, she spoke out for Jade Goody. 'Jade's a scapegoat,' she said. 'The other two are worse. Jade is someone who will walk down the street and people will either boo or give her a hug. But the other two, they will be pelted. If I was in the house, I'd kick their heads in.'

Rather amazingly, given quite what a big name she'd

become, when Amy and a group of friends, including Jamie Cullum, Michael Ball, and Craig Cash, grouped around the piano to sing at The Savoy hotel's American bar, they were asked to leave for being too rowdy. They had, in fact, trooped upstairs from the main ballroom, the location for the South Bank Show Awards, where Amy was proving she had staying power. She had flown from New York to Cannes and from there straight on to the awards, but managed to keep going, explaining, 'I've only just flown back to England today and have had hardly any sleep. My boyfriend is so whacked he has passed out.'

She herself was made of sterner stuff, and changed from her glamorous awards dress to jeans and a t-shirt, before gathering with her other famous friends at the bar. There was, as ever, a pianist in residence, and the group asked if they could join in: they did so, with Amy singing eight songs including 'They Can't Take That Away From Me', before the impromptu concert was brought to a halt. Even so, it all added to the glamour and the allure.

An insight into the world of Amy came when *The Observer* newspaper ran a food and drink special, detailing the eating habits – and a great deal more – about well-known celebrities of the day. It seemed that Amy, who had still not yet linked up with Blake, was off drugs at the time. Indeed, she almost sounded as if she was on a health kick. 'I stopped smoking weed about two years ago when I started going to the gym,' she recounted. 'Because I guess I've written "Addicted" and it's come out on this album [*Back to Black*], it would seem like I still smoke and have days where I think, "Oh, should I buy a quarter?" But it's not even a factor any more. I wrote that song about three years ago.'

She was candid, however, about the fact that, like so many addicts, she had replaced one problem with another. 'My drinking replaced weed,' she admitted. 'I still have a problem – well, I have had problems with drink, but I haven't had a drink in a few days. Is the problem exaggerated in the papers? I don't know. No. I'm a terrible drunk. I dunno where that comes from – boredom?'

It was an insightful remark. The intensely creative often carry an intensely self-destructive streak, and it may well be because they get bored so much more quickly than everyone else. But Amy was on the verge of letting it get totally out of control, something she couldn't yet see.

She was, however, adamant that her weight loss was nothing to worry about. 'No, I didn't drop four dress sizes to size zero,' she said. 'Size zero is an Americanism; it's not even a real English term. It'd be like a UK size four, which I've never been. At my smallest, I was an American size two, which is a six in the UK. But I was never even a twelve, so I dropped two dress sizes. It's a joke. It just makes me laugh when people say things like, "you were a spokeswoman for curvy girls, and you were a really good role model – and now look at you, you're a state..." I'm like, "What, I used to smoke weed from fucking eight o'clock in the morning until three o'clock in the morning. And when I stopped and started going to the gym, I lost a bit of weight and looked better – but I'm a terrible role model?" It's a joke.'

She did have a point. But of course, it wasn't just the weight loss that so concerned so many people; it was the fact that her drinking was getting so out of control. Amy, however, presented a different picture: one of healthy living as far as food was concerned. 'I eat ridiculously healthily,' she said. 'Just now I'm drinking a carrot, beetroot, celery, and ginger throat juice – it's gross. I'm gonna have red poo. But I've got to; I'm not well. I came back from Miami after New Year with a bug. My boyfriend Alex is a chef, and he can cook anything. But he doesn't cook for me; I cook for him. I do great chicken soup, or meatballs. But West Indian food is probably my best thing. I learnt from my mum, but she stopped cooking when I was quite young, so then I learnt from my grandma. I'm very enthusiastic about it.'

She was also, at that stage at least, very aware of the

importance of looking after her voice. Alex, who sounded like one of her more sensible boyfriends, was on hand to give advice. 'I love being on tour, and I do tend to look after my voice,' said Amy. 'One of my crew makes me really nice ginger tea. And Alex always tells me to avoid dairy – I was gonna get a smoothie with yoghurt in it, but he told me not to 'cause of my voice. When I was smoking a lot of weed I didn't have a munchie diet so much as I just ate badly. I'd get up, smoke two big spliffs then be like, "hmmm, I should eat something..." So I'd go and have a fry-up. Then I wouldn't eat anything all day. Then I'd eat pasta at two in the morning. Just ridiculous.'

She had given all that up and – drinking aside – it was all looking rosy. But Amy was to have a tumultuous time in the following months, with her private life totally overshadowing her music and marriage – now not far off.

A fresh-faced and innocent Amy Winehouse
at five years of age.

Amy signing copies of her first album, *Frank*, at
London's Virgin Megastore in December 2003.
Looking happy and healthy, this is a stark contrast to
how Amy would look in just a few short years.

A sultry and sexy Amy performing at the Brit Awards
Nominations Launch at London's Hyde Park Lane
Hotel in January 2004.

(*Above*) Amy poses with other music heavy weights, Jay Kay and Missy Elliott, in London, February 2004.

(*Right*) Amy at the Viva Glam V Lipstick and Lip Gloss Campaign, February 2004.

(Above) Amy's star begins to shine – at the Mercury Music Awards in 2004, where she won the Album of the Year.

(Right) Amy sporting the beehive that would become almost as famous as her music.

(*Left*) Amy poses at the Q Awards in October 2006. Her weight loss here is obvious, though it was to get worse.

(*Below*) One of the only calming influences in her life, Mitch Winehouse, Amy's father, poses proudly with his daughter at the Q Awards.

Amy at the Elle Style Awards in 2007 with friend and
fellow party girl, Kelly Osbourne.

Amy with her future husband, Blake Fielder-Civil,
the man many people believe has encouraged Amy's
wild lifestyle.

Queen Of Mean

THE EARLY months of 2007 were looking good for Amy. *Back to Black* eventually slipped off the number one slot, but had been a magnificent success and continued to dominate the music scene. Newcomer Lily Allen had, according to some, posed a threat to Amy as the outspoken bad girl of pop (or jazz), a challenge Amy saw off neatly when it was announced that she, and not Lily, would be performing at the Brits. This caused ructions in some quarters, with speculation that Lily might not now attend at all. She had been nominated for four awards, more than anyone else – Best Female, Best Album, Best Single, and Best Newcomer – but quite clearly was worried that Amy would upstage her.

'Lily is seriously considering staying away from the Brits,' said a source. 'She has a lot of commitments abroad so would have to make a special effort to fly in just for the day to go to the event. She was thrilled to be nominated in so many categories but many experts think she could lose out in all four. As soon as she was replaced by Amy

Winehouse on the roster of performers, people started saying, "There's no way she will win Best Female now – it will go to Winehouse." The Best Album category is so tough this year and she's got little chance of beating Arctic Monkeys. Best single is likely to go to Leona Lewis or Take That, and The Kooks are favourite to pick up the Newcomer award.' Amy herself, aware that this was an important performance, made it known that she intended to stay sober. There were to be no embarrassing 'Beat It'-style antics that night.

Amy was still continuing to party, though. There were reports that she and Kelly Osbourne had managed to spend £3,000 during one pub-crawl – although that did include clothes and food – ending the spree by doling out cups of tea to the homeless. The press loved it: if nothing else, she was a breath of fresh air in an industry that sometimes seemed so aware of the media, it dreaded causing offence.

And she continued to do the industry circuit. Amy showed up at the Meteor Ireland Music Awards, sporting a bigger beehive than ever but remaining well behaved. It was, it must be said, Amy's kind of night: 'The stars are coming to town to enjoy a big boozy Dublin night,' said a source. 'They won't be watching the show in the arena unless they go in briefly to collect an award. As soon as the formalities are completed they will be whisked straight back to the bar where unlimited booze has been laid on. There is a private pub at the Point next to the backstage area and it will be heaving with stars on the night. It's a recipe for a wild night and by the time the stars actually hit the clubs there will be a lot of tipsy celebrities around.'

The presenters, Podge and Rodge (who were appearing with the comedienne Deirdre O'Kane), were certainly looking forward to it. 'I'd like to try to tame that Amy Winehouse one,' said Rodge, a little unrealistically, but in the event it was a good-natured show. Amy behaved well, despite a bit of trouble with her microphone, but scarpered from the post-bash party at Spirit shortly afterwards to go and play pool.

'Amy and her band were in Spirit for a while but they weren't too keen on the music,' said a source. 'They ordered two bottles of champagne for Amy and the rest of the crew. But they weren't too impressed with the venue and decided to go off in search of the Kaiser Chiefs. A few bands were heading down to Eamon Doran's and Amy decided to go there instead. She had a much better time playing pool and hanging out – she's a down-to-earth girl really.'

Amy was still prone to flying off the handle at every opportunity. She startled onlookers at a television recording of *Later With Jools Holland* by letting rip at Kooks frontman Luke Pritchard after he had actually paid her a compliment. 'All I said to her was that I enjoyed her latest album,' said a slightly bewildered Luke. 'And suddenly, out of the blue, she had a massive go at me. At one point she told me to fucking pull my head out of my arse. It was really weird. Everyone was just standing around looking at her.'

'It's strange because she was really nice to begin with. But when I went up to her at the photoshoot she suddenly turned really cold. She's crackers.'

But Luke clearly had a strong streak of forgiveness. 'I fucking don't give a shit,' he said. 'Some people are just like that – artists such as Van Morrison, who's really moody. I still think she's great. I didn't really like her first album but I love her second. She's got an amazing voice.'

The various rivalries continued. Lily Allen decided she would, after all, go to the Brits, as her father, Keith Allen, said she had to. 'I really was going to stay away from the Brits because, as soon as the nominations came out, I knew that I wouldn't win anything,' she said. 'There's the split vote thing going on when you are nominated in all those categories, but I think Amy Winehouse will win the Best Female award and I don't think I will get anything. I'm away on tour during the week of the Brits, so I thought I'd just stay away for it and not be a bad loser. It's not like the end of the world if I don't win something. But when my dad found out I wasn't going, he went mad. He said it would be bad form. I tell you what, it comes to something when I've got to take etiquette lessons from my dad.'

But behind the scenes there were ructions, starting with problems with Alex. Then there were the forthcoming Brit awards. It was easy to see why Amy kept getting led astray: all her friends seemed to be queuing up to talk about drinking with her. Here is Matt Willis, hoping that Amy would help him stay off the drink at the awards: 'People label us pissheads, but there are other people our age drinking much more than us,' he said, before adding, 'We are a bad influence on each other.'

And here is James Morrison, who was also going to be attending the Brits, speaking hours before a concert in Amsterdam: 'I'm playing the biggest show of my life tonight – it's terrifying. I'm going to have a few drinks before I go on stage to calm the nerves. But I'm meeting up with Amy Winehouse later and she's mental and we're going to go on the lash together. We're planning to go to a few coffee shops and have a good smoke and get wasted – why not? We're here so we should make the most of it, but I just don't think I'll be able to keep up with her. I don't think I'll be visiting any prostitutes though!'

In that company, was it any wonder that Amy was prone to excess? Of course, all were young, recently successful, and being made a huge fuss of by an industry not known for its restraint; but it was a dangerous situation to be in without any steadying influences. And Amy was showing real signs of careening out of control. Her contribution to the Amsterdam trip was to remark, 'I might stock up on some porn while I'm out there – if I get the time. I haven't got that saucy latex nurse's uniform any more. I just borrowed that off my friend when I was a teenager – so maybe one of those as well.' Should she wear it to the Brits? 'Yeah, maybe,' she said. 'I haven't actually sorted out anything to wear for it yet.'

Amy had, of course, been extremely open about her drug taking in the past. How, she was asked, was she going to cope with a place like Amsterdam? 'I might have a smoke over there, but it's just not a big deal for me any more,' she said. 'If someone's got one on the go I'll have a pull or two. But I don't rely on it any more. I just got sick of it, you know? And I haven't really been out drinking that often recently because I've been working so much. It means that when I do go out with my mates, I don't want to get too hammered because I'm so grateful to be with them and I don't want to spoil a good night. Sometimes I do have one too many and get out of my pram, though.'

And she was still with Alex. 'I was up early this morning to make a chilli con carne for my boyfriend and his mate so they could have a nice lunch before I went away,' she said.

'I'm probably going to take him to the Brits with me. He's my best friend. I'll take him and my old man. My dad's like my awards show sidekick now. He'll just go up to someone like Pete Townshend and tell him he hates his cufflinks or something. He's just so real and always has such a good time.'

And even Amy admitted to being excited by the upcoming Brits. 'I don't know if I'll win, but I guess winning one for best album would be the ultimate,' she said. 'Arctic Monkeys will get that, though. I'm performing "Rehab" with the band. The Brits people didn't ask me to do anything special or to duet with anyone, so I'll just do my usual thing. I'll have the odd drink but I won't be going overboard – unless I go to the Oasis after-party, in which case it could all get a little bit blurry.'

The awards still rolled in. In February, Amy won the best British music act at the Elle Style Awards, declaring her style icon to be, 'my nan', although she did cause concern because of her appearance. One arm was covered in red marks. The Brits were up next. Lily Allen had clearly decided to be magnanimous towards her rival (while laying into another.) 'Corinne Bailey Rae?' she said. 'I think she's a bit boring, sorry. She's a lovely girl but I don't think her music stands out and I'd be a bit annoyed if she won. I'd be really happy if Amy Winehouse wins, though. She's brilliant.'

And Amy was being as generous about Lily Allen as Lily had been to her. 'It's going to be Lily's year,' she said. 'She came out of nowhere and whacked everyone over the head with a frying pan. I really don't think I'm going to get anything, so I won't be preparing any speeches. But that doesn't matter – I'll be excited whatever happens. It's Valentine's Day as well, so just being with my boyfriend will be enough reason for a celebration. He is the most beautiful man I've ever seen.

In fact, they were shortly going to break up, but there was no sign of it yet. 'Usually, he walks out and I end up following him down the road,' said Amy, admitting the couple rowed a lot. 'But I love spoiling him and buying him presents. My idea of heaven is to have the time to clean my house and cook for him. Our relationship is going really well but we're definitely not ready for wedding bells. We're still only babies ourselves.'

Amy was being her usual self as the Brits approached. 'Yes, I'm still going to misbehave!' she assured one interviewer. 'My new thing is to try to do one night on, one night off,' she said. 'But that doesn't mean I've been going for colonics every day. Because of the job I do and the industry I'm in, there's just so much opportunity to go out every night and get smashed.'

There was also still the possibility of that much-mooted

duet with Pete Doherty, although Amy played it down. 'It would be cool but he's all over the shop and so am I,' she said. 'We're as flaky as each other, so I wouldn't hold your breath for it. Basically, I live to do gigs; it's my life and I can't wait for the Glastonbury and V festivals. I've also had offers to do modelling and stuff. But I'm like, are they mad? I'm not exactly an oil painting, am I?'

Certainly no one else saw her that way. Russell Brand, the only other person in show business with hair to match Amy's, remarked, 'I'm challenging the lovely Amy Winehouse to a backcombing battle at the Brits tonight. I'm planning to grow my hair to the size of a nuclear mushroom cloud in anticipation.' He certainly seemed to find Amy attractive; as did a good many of the men she met. She just didn't notice.

Rather touchingly, Amy took both her parents to the awards ceremony. According to the singer, however, this was not going to hamper her style. 'My dad is on a mission to get drunk because he hardly ever drinks normally as he's driving,' she said as she arrived in a little yellow number. 'But tonight he's going to celebrate. He'll certainly show Liam and Noel [Gallagher] what partying is all about! He's on my table and the two of us are going to be joined at the hip. I'll make sure he does plenty of partying!'

Although she had been famous for some time now,

Amy was not coming across as the big-headed diva – indeed, those frequent remarks about how unattractive she was showed her to be nothing of the sort. Instead, she seemed rather thrilled by it all. 'It's amazing to be on The Brits,' she said. 'I used to watch it all the time when I was a kid and I always wanted to be on the show but I never thought I'd make it. I remember seeing Take That on it and I was completely in love with Mark Owen and Robbie Williams, so it's wicked Mark is on the same Brits as me.'

Robbie, of course, wasn't actually present, as he'd announced he'd checked himself into rehab to combat an addiction to prescription pills. 'I feel gutted for him,' said Amy. 'Addiction to prescription drugs is a really hard thing. I hope he comes out okay. I've always had a soft spot for him.'

She herself felt no need to do likewise. 'I'm much more sorted than I have been for a long time,' she said. 'I'm completely in love with my man and my work is going really well. I'm doing some fantastic gigs. On top of that I'm pretty happy with the way I look.'

In the event, Amy won the British Female Solo Artist award, receiving it from the Radio 1 DJ, Jo Whiley. 'Sorry, what can I say? Thank you very much,' she said. 'I've worked very hard and had a lot of help. I'm glad my mum and dad are here, to be honest. I just put on my sexiest dress and hoped.' It was a rather poignant reminder of how young she still was.

Onlookers were also alarmed to see scars on her arm, which a spokesman said were due to a drunken fall in New York: 'I probably walked around the block trying to get to the hotel and fell,' said Amy. 'I have no idea. I hate that. The blackouts. Happens too often.' The papers, meanwhile, went to town: 'Singer who refused rehab crowned Queen of the Brits' was one headline.

Costume changes were the order of the night. After arriving in yellow, Amy changed into red to sing 'Rehab' because her first dress 'clashes with the fucking set' she announced. (The carpet was red.) Then it was another change into black and white to collect the award. At the party afterwards, Amy was still appearing a bit dazed. 'I can't believe it, I'm over the moon,' she said, although she certainly hadn't lost her sense of humour. Backstage, the area was decorated as a 'decadent love-fest tattoo parlour,' with red walls and gothic candlesticks, along with a life-sized stuffed ewe. Amy shoved a cigarette in its mouth.

The evening itself was enlivened by the presence of Russell Brand, the presenter, while the show itself went out live in an attempt to inject some excitement into the proceedings. Russell himself was responsible for livening things up: he pointed to a large padlock behind him:

'Robbie Williams's medicine cabinet,' he announced. He then continued, 'Let Me Entertain You – as long as you don't get sixty fags, twenty Redbulls, and some happy pills to get into the mood. Robbie is a hero of the Brits. If we send him our love he will hear it. Get well England's rose. One day at a time old bean.' The crowd cheered.

Meanwhile, Lily Allen, who had been coaxed into coming and who had, indeed, won nothing, was gracious about it all. 'I knew I wasn't going to win, but I'm happy to be here,' she said.

The award put Amy into a whole new league, with a real possibility of now cracking America. *Back to Black*, which by now had sold over 700,000 copies, had slipped down the charts to number five, but in the wake of her win, bounced up to number two. Gennaro Castaldo, of HMV, was in no doubt what it meant. 'Aside from the kudos that it gives you, winning a Brit or performing at the awards ceremony can seriously enhance an artist's recording career,' he said. 'The endorsement and profile that it gives you means that successful artists can break out of their immediate fan base to connect with a much wider, more mainstream audience. This is happening right now to Amy Winehouse. It will help take her to that next level of stardom, as we have seen in the past with the likes of Robbie Williams and Coldplay.' It was heady stuff.

Alas, the good feeling behind the various rivals didn't last. At the Brits itself, a fan told Lily Allen she should have won, rather than Amy: 'I fucking know,' she (loudly) replied. Matters swiftly deteriorated. She had another argument with a photographer, before having a go at Amy herself. 'I had a real slanging match with Amy Winehouse,' she admitted the next day. 'We had a really bad row. It was terrible.'

It also seemed to have affected her badly. The next day, Lily was seen in tears at Heathrow airport on her way to Washington DC, and it seemed the spat was on her mind. 'She had tears streaming down her face and she seemed as though she hadn't slept a wink,' said an onlooker. 'She looked really rough and hungover. Someone asked if she was all right and she said she'd had a bust-up with Amy Winehouse. She was sniffing and wiping tears from her cheeks. She looked like a little lost schoolgirl.'

And it wasn't just Amy she was scrapping with. Jon Fratelli, who won the Best British Breakthrough Act award recounted that she had a go at him, too. 'I was talking to Liam when Lily started yelling at me,' he related. 'Apparently we "robbed" her and I'm a "cunt" for doing so – she was really pissed off. I just laughed. But Lily's dad had to lift her out of the room, kicking and screaming. He shouted at her, "Right child, it's time you went home to bed." It was a spectacular strop.'

Lily herself seemed a little embarrassed in retrospect. 'Amy and I are friends,' she said rather more diplomatically, a couple of days later. 'I always said that if I wasn't going to win then I hoped she did. I'm very pleased for her. I was in tears the next day because I hardly get to see [her boyfriend] Seb and I was leaving to get on yet another plane.' Jon did not get a mention.

Interest in Amy, already strong, intensified after the Brits. Of course it was her bad habits – the boozing, the scars – that really aroused everyone's curiosity, and now her father Mitch clearly decided it was time for him to speak up for his wayward, but colossally talented child. 'She had just split up with her boyfriend and had a lot to drink,' he said of another occasion when she'd fallen over and hurt herself. 'She fell over and bumped her head. Her friends phoned me and I went down to her flat. I said, "You're coming home with me." Her previous management company said she should go to rehab, but she didn't think she needed to, and I agreed. I told her I thought she looked okay. She was lovesick. You can't go to rehab for that. I don't think she is an alcoholic. If you're an alcoholic you drink every day.'

Nor was he happy about stories about her drug use. 'My daughter isn't drug-crazed,' he said. 'Even when I was a young man I dabbled – what young person hasn't?'

He accepted, though, that one of her songs, 'What Is It About Men', was partly about him. 'What she writes is true to life, and sometimes it's painful,' he said. '"What Is It About Men" was fair enough. She didn't lie about it – she wrote, "All the shit my mother went through". It was true. I did put her mother through a lot of shit. But I was only unfaithful to her once.'

Mitch was also aware of Amy's problems with food. 'She's had these spells with eating problems – an eating disorder,' he said. 'When she recorded her first album three years ago she had a nice figure, a nice cleavage, I thought she looked great. But she doesn't like that look. Six months ago she was really skinny, but she's fine now. I went out with her the other day and she had a normal meal. She looks after herself, goes to the gym, and eats healthily. She always liked salads. But she obviously has a distorted view of herself.'

He was not, however, so keen on the tattoos. 'I don't like them – but if I said something she would just say, "I'm twenty-three",' he said.

As for the future, Mitch was extremely positive. 'Her album's coming out in the States next month and she is going on the David Letterman show,' he said. 'She wants to make it over there. She recently asked me for a couple of hundred quid. But I don't mind – she hasn't seen all the money she's due yet.'

The Morning After

IN THE AFTERMATH of the Brit awards, Amy was riding high, pleased with the acknowledgement of her peers, and in extremely good odour with her record company. Meanwhile, Lily Allen was doing her absolute utmost to mend any bridges, and was again emphasising that her airport tears had nothing to do with Amy or the Brits and everything to do with a brief separation from her boyfriend.

'The story about me being in tears either because I didn't win a Brit or had a fight with Amy is complete rubbish,' she said. 'She and I are friends and we were hanging out at the Brits and at the Oasis party afterwards. I was talking to her and Mark Ronson for ages. Mark is a mutual friend who produced Amy's album and mine. I always said that I wasn't expecting to win, and that if I wasn't going to win then I hoped Amy did. I'm very pleased for her. The pictures of me crying in the papers were taken when I was saying goodbye to my boyfriend, who I haven't seen much of recently. I've been working really hard and travelling a lot and I only got to see him at the Brits so the tears were just because I was leaving to get on yet another plane.'

Unfortunately, however, just as Amy should have been celebrating the biggest triumph of her career, her behind-the-scenes problems took a sharp turn for the worse. Everyone knew Amy drank in industrial quantities; everyone knew she had dabbled in drugs in the past. But she had never had a problem with hard drugs, saying at one point in the past, 'Cocaine isn't really my thing.' Now, however, it was beginning to look as if it was. She was photographed leaving a post-Brits party with what looked like traces of white powder around her nostrils.

'It was late and Amy was totally off her face, but somehow she still had loads of energy,' said a witness to the scene. 'She was jiggling around and whistling to herself. When she got in the cab she started wiping her nose furiously. Everyone knows she's one of the biggest caners on the scene at the moment, but if she's getting into Class As, it's bad news.'

Amy herself point-blank denied there was a problem. 'I'm over that stuff now,' she said. 'I've got nothing to hide and I've never pretended to be perfect. Everyone likes a drink and I'm no different. What is different is that people take pictures of me when I'm hammered so I don't get away with it. But I have so little time with my friends these days that when I do get a chance to go out with them I don't want to get so out of my pram that I can't remember it the next day.'

As for the drugs: 'Any problems I've had haven't been caused by cocaine, despite what people have said,' said Amy. 'When I split up with my last boyfriend, I was doing a few drugs, but only dabbling. Cocaine isn't really my thing and I was never really on it and it's not a big deal to me. I'd rather be at home with my fella cooking, or seeing my family, or just playing pool and having a quiet drink in my local.'

But whether it had been her thing or not, it was certainly becoming so. Amy, with her reckless drinking and admitted fondness for soft drugs was, alas, a prime target for the harder stuff, especially in an industry such as the music one. The danger signs as to what were about to happen were all there: far from bringing her excessive behaviour under control, Amy was allowing it to get completely out of hand.

But that was not yet obvious to everyone else. 'Sure, there's loads of instrumental passages nicked from girlie groups, but Amy, bless her mutilated little stick-insect body and horrific taste in eye make-up, is a thoroughly addictive and engaging performer,' wrote Janet Street-Porter. 'Our songstresses are strutting their stuff in a way we authors can only dream of,' said the Australian author Kathy Lette. 'Winehouse and Allen don't just walk on the wild side; they positively sprint. And in high heels, too.' True enough – but Amy was going to take a mighty tumble.

Was Amy in denial? Very possibly. 'I don't really have a problem with alcohol,' she reiterated in an interview a couple of days after The Brits. 'I have a problem with me that probably comes out when I drink. I try to please everybody all the time and then it all builds up. I get frustrated. Oh, I don't know. What do I know anyway?'

But she was beginning to realize the effect this was having on her family. 'I was sitting on the tube this morning reading a newspaper. I saw this piece about myself and I got a bit embarrassed, so I closed it quick,' she said. 'I didn't want anybody to notice I was reading about myself. It doesn't really bother me. It's all water off a duck's back. People around me might get shit for it. My boyfriend's mum keeps telling him I have a drink problem – she says she read it in the newspaper and tells him that he's got to tell me to stop drinking. It's embarrassing. People at work are saying to her that her "daughter-in-law" is an alcoholic.'

'It's also tough on my parents because they are protective of me. It must be hard for respectable people. When I went to rehab – not one of those posh ones, this one was out in the sticks – this fellow told me I was not an alcoholic, and so I went home. I think what helped was that when I went to the rehab interview I did my hair all nice – perfect make-up, high heels, nice jeans, smart jacket – and the man took one look at me and thought, "You really don't look like you need any help." I know it's not really all about how you look, but I didn't look weedy and ill. I was drinking a lot. I'd be ill for a couple of days – but I would bounce back because at the time I was training at the gym.'

Amy was also very clear about the debt she owed to Mark Ronson. That eighteen-month quiet spell, after the success of *Frank*, had been because of the problems in her personal life, and it was Ronson who picked her up after that. He even provided her with one of her most famous lines. 'I was telling him about how I'd hit rock bottom, when my ex-boyfriend Blake left me broken-hearted and they tried to get me into rehab,' she recounted. 'He was laughing disbelievingly, saying, "No, no, no!"'

Preparations were now in full swing for her to take America by storm: a gig had been booked at the Bowery Ballroom, and she was due to appear on David Letterman. She also seemed to be pulling herself together, appearing at the London Astoria (the same stage she had to leave after her all-day binge with Kelly Osbourne), for the Shockwaves NME Awards show. Amy acknowledged as much.

'The last time I was here I didn't manage too many

songs,' she told the crowd. 'I've done a bit better this time and I should give myself a pat on the back.' The audience adored it. 'Don't worry, Amy, we love you!' someone cried from the back, as she put in a cracker of a performance that even had the audience singing along. She was clearly relieved at the end of the gig. 'Last time I was here, I only got through six songs, so I pat myself on the back,' she said again. 'I thought there would be a lot of angry homosexuals on the door.'

With that, Amy was off, playing more dates around the UK. She was also signed up for that summer's T in the Park – and much was made of the fact that Lily Allen was also going to be there. 'Lily Allen is a great girl to get with some great sounds as well,' said promoter Geoff Ellis. 'And we are really pleased to get Amy Winehouse. She will give Lily Allen a run for her money at the backstage bar.'

Of course, Amy was becoming quite the seasoned traveller by now, and was being asked for her tips for jetting about the world. In an interview with *The Observer* she said, 'Take a pillow from home. I was gutted to leave my boyfriend at home when I started my tour, but taking my pillow was like taking a little bit of him with me.'

Amy had also developed some rather eccentric habits when she was abroad. Asked what she always returned with, she replied, 'Chewing gum. I've got a drawer in my house full of it. I must get through about four packs a day. I don't smoke that much, so I guess I chew gum instead. In America they've got this really good Trident gum that is sweet and sour. It's strawberry-flavour, sugar-free, and comes twelve to a pack. Six sticks are sweet and six are sour. I have an ongoing gum-off competition with one of the guys from my band over who can find the weirdest gum when we're on tour!'

Nor was Amy an intellectually challenged pop star, showing herself to be a voracious reader. 'I read a lot when I'm travelling and always have a couple of books on the go,' she said. 'I read all sorts of stuff, but this week I bought an anthology of graphic fiction, because I love graphic novels and cartoons, and another copy of *Carter Beats the Devil* by Glen David Gold – a great novel. I also bought Alexei Sayle's *Barcelona Plates*, which I'm looking forward to reading. I could spend a lot of time in bookshops just browsing.'

And she was also beginning to travel in style. Who was the last person she sat beside? 'My boyfriend,' said Amy. 'We got to fly first-class. I drank water because you get so dehydrated on the plane and get off looking like a raisin, but he was drinking champagne and got quite giggly – it was funny! I'm lucky because I do get to fly first-class now. I'm not that bothered and won't make a fuss, but my manager is so tall he needs the legroom.'

Amy had been gaining plaudits for her shows across Britain and Ireland, for their sleekness, professionalism, and the fact that she was clearly staying off the booze – when she was onstage, at least. But then, she suddenly and unexpectedly cancelled a gig at the Shepherd's Bush Empire – Sir Elton John was due to have been in the audience – due to 'unforeseen circumstances.' Her management said she was ill, but with a record like hers, of course, there were suspicions that all was far from well.

There was a bit of light relief when it was announced that Amy would be recording a duet of the Ronettes' hit 'Be My Baby', entitled 'B Boy Baby', with one of the other great eccentrics of the pop scene, ex-Sugababe Mutya Buena. 'Amy and Mutya have a lot in common and have talked about collaborating for a while,' said a source. 'As labelmates it's easy to sort that out and Amy's involvement will give her a real kick-start. Because Amy's managed to make that old-fashioned sound popular again, they weren't scared to give it a real Sixties feel. The video will be great.'

She certainly needed something to take her mind off things, because the reason for the cancelled gig suddenly became clear: in early March, she and Alex split up. Amy did as she always did and hit the bottle: first she was seen shopping for wine in her local supermarket. 'Her eyes were glazed over and we thought it was because she was drunk,' said an onlooker. 'When we heard about the split we realised she could have been crying.'

She then went to a party at the Griffin Pub, in Shoreditch, East London, where she was overheard yelling, 'What are you fucking looking at?' before ending up at the K-West Hotel in Shepherd's Bush. There was no mistaking that she was the worse for wear. 'Amy staggered all over the place, looking really upset,' said a source. 'Her friend was saying Amy had split up with her boyfriend Alex and had been drinking since the night before.'

There was, briefly, talk of a reunion. Amy was due to fly out to the States, and there was speculation Alex would join her there. 'New York is their favourite place to go as a couple,' said a friend. 'The last time they had a massive row, Amy had to go out there to work on Mark Ronson's new album and she took Alex with her. They made up and spent most of their time there in the sack.'

But it was not to be. Amy issued various statements saying she felt fine, but was pictured in New York looking anything but. She made it on stage at the Bowery Ballroom and received a rapturous reception from fans, before going on to the South by Southwest live music festival in Austin, Texas, where she completely stole the show.

In fact, Amy's trip to the States was a massive success. The music industry loved her and so did the fans: her album *Back to Black* entered the US album chart at number seven, the most successful debut ever by a British woman in the Billboard Hot 100. The only hiccup came when a Los Angeles showcase had to be cancelled due to technical difficulties (and there really were technical difficulties). Amongst those said to be impressed by her talent and her voice were Bruce Willis and Justin Timberlake: the future could not have looked rosier. Even the Rolling Stones were impressed, inviting her to duet with them at that year's Isle of Wight festival.

Back in Britain, however, the real reason for Amy's break-up with Alex was becoming clear. Blake was back on the scene, and there had been a huge bust-up after Alex had caught them at the end of an all day boozing session. 'They looked like they had been partying hard,' said a friend. 'Her old man had been looking for her all day. He dragged her out and put her in a cab. Blake was left looking sorry for himself and kept saying he was going to get the blame.'

Indeed, Blake Fielder-Civil, a runner on music videos, was now ready to go public with the relationship and reveal how very much he had been the inspiration behind *Back to Black*. They had only split up, according to Blake, because he had been unfaithful (hardly a good omen for the future); ominously, he was already up on a GBH charge.

'When we met we were attracted to each other instantly – and we've never stopped being that way,' he said. 'I know me and Amy are going to be together. She's the love of my life. In *Back To Black* the lyrics, "You go back to her, and I go back to black" is about that situation. And "You Know I'm No Good" is her retaliating to the fact I could not be with her.'

Well, he could now. The reconciliation was putting everything in a different light: Amy now confessed that those Shepherd's Bush gigs were cancelled not because of her broken heart, but because she fell on her face when she was drunk and lost a tooth. 'I broke a big tooth,' she admitted. 'I had a massive gap in the front of my mouth.' But she was determined to clean up. 'I love going on tour more than anything,' she said. 'It keeps me off the streets.'

Matters rapidly got more complicated. Amy was briefly reunited with Alex, but it didn't last, and soon she and Blake were enmeshed in each other again. It was hardly surprising that she admitted to suffering from depression at this juncture, confessing that she would sometimes slap herself in the face.

'Not punching myself in the face, but slapping,' she continued. 'I drank a whole bottle of champagne and then just got depressed. I didn't feel like I looked good. And I'm quite self-destructive when I'm drunk.' As for her tattoos, now numbering thirteen, they were also a way of making her feel. 'It's a way of suffering for the things that mean a lot to you,' she said. 'Actually I like the pain. To me, it relieves you.'

It didn't exactly speak of a calm frame of mind. Her emotional life was chaos: the reconciliation with Alex was extremely short-lived, and in no time she was back with Blake. Unfortunately, whereas Alex seemed to calm her down, Blake did exactly the opposite and Amy's emotional life grew ever more dramatic, with reports of rows with both her ex and current beaus. She was drinking more than ever; it wouldn't be long before she was experimenting with ever-harder drugs.

She was still fulfilling her other obligations, however. Her producer, Mark Ronson, had just recorded an album of his own, *Version*, and Amy was one of the star vocalists who guested on it. Others were Lily Allen and Robbie Williams, whom he also produced. She also had just released the single of *Back to Black*, and was garnering the usual rave reviews. But it was her behaviour that continued to fascinate most, as when she did a gig at London's G-A-Y club and was offered a bottle of champagne or a bunch of flowers at the end of her performance. Amy opted for the latter, saying, 'I don't drink.' There was also great excitement when she was spotted feeding lemurs at Bristol Zoo.

But all of this paled into insignificance in late April. Amy had spent some time to-ing and fro-ing between Blake and Alex, but now Blake had well and truly won the day. He proposed, was accepted, and the happy couple wasted no time in telling everyone the news. 'I am so pleased Blake proposed. It's fucking amazing, fantastic!' she told the *Daily Star*. 'Look at my ring! I'm ecstatic!'

'This is the real deal and ecstatic isn't the word,' Blake added.

To another paper, she said, 'We are very close and the best of friends. I don't want to be with anyone else and nor does he. I am a very lucky girl to have found someone I love a lot. I want to be with Blake for the rest of my life. He proposed at home a few days ago and I took a day to finally agree. Obviously we are both young and it is frightening. But it is the right thing to do. That is why I agreed.'

Blake, meanwhile, said, 'We are both delighted. It is nice to have some happy news when there is so much stuff happening in America.'

The 'stuff' he was referring to was Amy's astonishing success in America. It was really looking as if she had a huge future over there – but even at this early stage, some people expressed concern about the effect Blake might have on this. He was, after all, facing a charge of GBH, and he was also as reckless about substance abuse as Amy herself. Clearly the couple adored one another, but at the same time there were fears they would drive each other to ever-greater excess. Those fears were to prove spot on.

At that stage, however, it seemed churlish to worry, and Amy had other things on her mind. Despite her frequent references to herself as being unattractive, the knowledge that she was widely scene as a sex symbol in many quarters didn't seem to please her either. 'It should be about the music and not about how many tats I have or the size of my boobs, should it?' she demanded.

At least she still had Juliette. Although Amy was now very famous, the friendship hadn't wavered: the two were as close as ever. Asked if Amy's fame had changed anything, Juliette replied, 'No, from day one we've always had the same kind of goals, ambitions. I sing, and I write songs as well, and to be able to see her making a success of it brought us closer together. There's no jealousy there. Some of her other friends started acting a bit weird and starstruck. But if I see Amy on TV, I just think, "Oh, there's Amy the Dickhead again."'

One person who was not taking that attitude was Alex. He was clearly livid that Amy had chosen Blake over him, and was making no secret of his dismay. 'I'm skint, heartbroken, and homeless,' he complained. 'After turning up at three in the morning at The Hawley Arms, I saw the ex with her ex and I saw red mist. I was shaking like a leaf and decided to fall off the wagon. I got leathered while she sat there inebriated and on the lap of her ex.'

Indeed, his habits were clearly not dissimilar to Amy's. 'A friend gave me a little something I hadn't had in a while – MDMA,' he continued. 'I always forget how enjoyable everything is after you taste that rank shit, especially with a couple of valium, three lines, and a little dark rum to wash it down. Although the future was looking bright, turns out, I was gravely mistaken. Skint, heartbroken, and homeless – bad luck comes in threes as the old saying goes, but shit, what's a man to do.'

The two had initially kept in touch, but Alex clearly wasn't able to any more. 'I had a nice day with my ex Amy, everything was sweet, then she went to some party and I found out she's with her ex,' he said. 'Life can have a way of kickin' you in the teeth. [I'm] trying to filter through all the bullshit and [I] can't write any more songs about the bitch, because I've covered all my emotions, so I'm gonna find myself a new muse.'

On another occasion, he sounded more bitter. 'She drinks way too much and misses out on meals,' he said. 'Her weight has plummeted so much it knocked me back a bit. Once, she kneed me in the bollocks. It got so bad we split three times. She always asked me back. She'd say, "I love you, it'll never happen again". And as far as Blake was concerned, she'd say they were over for good. The last time we were together she even promised she'd have the famous tattoo of his name on her left breast removed. It's like she cut out my heart, bit a chunk out of it, threw it on the floor, and stomped on it. She's scared to be happy. I hope she finds happiness one day. She needs looking after, but I'm glad that's not my responsibility any more.'

At least her other friends were sticking up for her. Her great pal and fellow bad behaviourist Kelly Osbourne was adamant that it was she and not Amy who put it away in heroic quantities: 'Amy isn't as bad as everyone says she is,' she said. 'I'm worse – but I'm good at hiding it.' Mark Ronson felt the same way. 'She gets me out of situations in a motherly way,' he said. 'Put it this way, she's often been the voice of reason on a couple of nights out.'

Meanwhile, Amy's career continued to soar: she was now nominated for Best Contemporary Song in the Ivor Novello awards for 'Rehab'. There was also the possibility that she would work with the hip hopper Jay Z: 'Jay Z told Amy he had some great ideas and when he called her back a few days later, she couldn't believe it,' said a source.

The American side of life was certainly going well.

Shortly after announcing her engagement to Blake, Amy arrived in LA for a short US tour, although she did excite comment because of how thin she'd become. Back in Britain, she was headlining at a number of music festivals during the summer: 'Wear shorts, not skirts, because ladies do tend to fall over,' she advised. She also proved to be an enormous draw at California's Coachella Valley Music and Arts Festival: A-listers including Drew Barrymore, Cameron Diaz, Danny de Vito, and her old mate Kelly Osbourne were all in attendance. 'I'm not really a confident person and I was really nervous,' she said afterwards. 'But as soon as my set was finished, I wanted to do it all over again. Then I met Danny DeVito backstage – and we're about the same size!'

While she was in the States, Amy established one rather bizarre friendship with a star almost as troubled as Amy was to become – Britney Spears. According to sources that witnessed the whole thing, they got on remarkably well. 'Britney was really keen to meet Amy after falling in love with her album *Back to Black*,' said one. 'Her people set up a meeting at the Sky Bar in LA and the girls really hit it off. Britney wants her new material to be more autobiographical and raw – something Amy really achieved with her recent work.'

'They got on so well they headed to new Hollywood club

Winston's to hang out. Britney wasn't drinking and Amy only had a couple. That's mainly because they couldn't stop chatting. Amy told Britney about her recent engagement. Britney said she was sure it would be a success as Amy had returned to the one true love of her life. She was really excited for her about it. Britney told Amy about her intimate gig at the House Of Blues and said it would be good to duet together at some point. She even suggested a road trip together under aliases.' It was bizarre, certainly – but not a patch on what actually was to come about.

Wedding Belle

SPRING 2007 seemed to be a good time for Amy. Whatever doubts her own parents might have had about her forthcoming marriage, her in-laws-to-be were delighted. Blake's mother Georgette said she was thrilled; his stepfather Giles added, 'A family wedding is a lovely idea. We like Amy very much.' There was even talk that Blake might convert to Judaism, although in the event a rather different set of nuptials took place.

Her career was certainly no cause for concern. Amazingly, *Back to Black*, which had slipped slightly in the charts, was on the way up again, now hitting number three. And she received acclaim from yet another quarter, this time the diminutive rock star Prince, who was due to play in London that summer and expressed the wish to duet with Amy. 'I love Amy's track "Love Is A Losing Game",' he said. 'We play that a lot. I'm a big fan. We're still sorting out the support acts, but if I saw her onstage I would absolutely ask her to join me.'

'I'm honoured,' replied Amy. 'I'm a massive fan. I'd love

to work with him. I hope I can do the gigs. I'll drop everything. Stuff like that makes me want to do it tomorrow and
the night after and the night after. Now I want to find out
how solid the offer is. I'd do it with bells on – all day long.'

She was then nominated for three awards in the Mojo
Honours List, an endorsement, if ever there was one, of
how far she'd come: 'Rehab' was up for Song of the Year;
Back to Black was up for Best Album, and Amy was nominated for Best Live Act. Meanwhile, her star continued
to shine ever more brightly in the United States. She and
Blake were frequently pictured in New York as her popularity across the pond continued to soar. Her album had
reached number seven in the US charts, an extraordinary
achievement. Her record company was certainly pleased:
'There's no one thing that accounts for Amy's success in
America,' said Hassan Choudhury, vice-president of international marketing at Universal Music UK. 'There is the
visual side, combined with all of the press interest in her –
combined with the fact that she has made a great record.'

There was also a great deal of speculation Amy would
appear in the next James Bond film, or at least perform the
title track, something that clearly amused her greatly. 'Can
you imagine me in Bond with Craig?' she asked. 'There's
no way I'd want to be good like a Bond babe, it'd have to
be bad.'

Bond producer Barbara Broccoli was said to be a fan. 'She has all the assets Barbara would want as a baddie in the next *Casino Royale*,' said a source. 'And everyone involved with this thinks that she is just perfect. She's a cool character who both young and old can relate to.'

In as much as she was thinking about the future, Amy was beginning to understand that all life experiences could be used towards her work. She cited her favourite group, the Shangri-Las. 'I realised,' she said, 'that the Shangri-Las have pretty much got a song for every stage of a relationship. When you see a boy and you don't even know his name. When you start talking to him. When you start going out with him. And then when you're in love with him. And then when he fucking chucks you and then you want to kill yourself.' It was, after all, how *Back to Black* had come about.

And an old rivalry reared its head when Lily Allen, clearly very fed up about something, wrote amongst other things, the following on a blog: 'I am fat, ugly, and shitter than Winehouse, that is all I am.' Amy couldn't resist a dig. 'Some people like Lily can't hack the pace of touring the States – but for me it's been great,' she said rather cattily. 'They are all so friendly in the States and above all they love my music.'

Amy also had other things on her mind. In mid-May,

she and Blake were spotted in Miami, leading to rumours that the couple was about to wed. Blake was seen getting clothes altered, while a very select group of friends was in attendance. 'They've been forced to leave their mobiles at home so that news of the wedding doesn't leak out,' said a source. Amy scoffed at the speculation about the clothes. 'Oh yeah – he just bought that suit in New York last week and didn't have a chance to alter it,' she said.

But news was beginning to leak quite fast. Amy herself was keen to quash the gossip: 'Nah, we're just chilling out, having a good time,' she said. 'We only just got engaged.' Two days later, news leaked out that the two had, in fact, tied the knot. 'Amy and Blake got married this morning,' said a spokesman. 'They are both very happy.' Blake lost no time in alerting the public to the state of affairs: he immediately changed his status on MySpace to 'married'. Mark Ronson sent the couple his good wishes. 'I'm so happy for her,' he said. 'She kept that under wraps.'

The wedding itself, which took place on 18 May 2007 in Miami, was an extremely private affair. 'Amy and Blake left their hotel room in the early hours of the morning and disappeared,' said a source. They quietly made their way to downtown Miami to the Miami Dade County marriage licence bureau, where they met deputy clerk Sammy Calixte, who married them. Amy was dressed in a short, halterneck print dress and Blake was in a Fifties-style suit. 'They came in this morning to get married and they were alone,' said Sammy. 'I read the marriage vows and each one said, "I do". When I pronounced them man and wife they hugged and kissed.'

The newly married pair returned to the Shore Club to celebrate with friends, after which they had a £6,000 celebration at the Delanos Hotel. When they returned to their room, a giggling Amy said, 'You've got to carry me in.' Blake duly obliged.

Everyone, including the friends who were in situ, was amazed. 'Everyone was sure Amy was going to tie the knot today but she's never been one to do what's expected,' said one. 'She was keen to make sure no one knew anything about it, so they could keep it quiet. But now the word is out that they are apparently husband and wife.'

Amy maintained a dignified silence, winking at journalists who were asking whether it could true, but Blake was a little more forthcoming. 'We had a great day,' he said. 'It's all cool.' The pair was certainly besotted with each other, kissing openly and frequently.

It was certainly a passionate relationship. The knot now well and truly tied, the pair spent the next two days in their hotel suite, occasionally calling on room service for sustenance. 'Amy told Blake that she'd spare no expense

– she's working so hard now that they tried to cram two weeks' worth of fun into two days,' said a friend. 'They locked themselves in and wouldn't even leave to let the chambermaids change the linen! Every few hours, they'd call and ask for bubbly and occasionally French fries. They seemed far more interested in booze than food!'

There were, as ever, some naysayers who looked askance at the whole business. Some people who knew the couple were genuinely concerned for their welfare and were worried that they might egg each other on to damage themselves. Others, rather more unpleasantly, questioned Blake's motives. 'Blake has been singing, "They tried to make me sign a pre-nup, but I said no, no, no" to the tune of her "Rehab" song,' said a friend. 'Some of the people that know him have nicknamed him Anna Nicole Smith because they think he's only after her money.'

Another friend also expressed doubts. 'I used to go out clubbing with Blake,' he said. 'He's kind of a charming bad boy. He's the sort of bloke who's got all the chat – who's got a little twinkle in his eye. He'll go out and misbehave and do who knows what, but he'd never let a woman go through a door second. He's always called a "music video assistant", or a "gopher" but I don't know about that. I don't know where he gets his money from.'

Others said that even when Amy had been with Alex, it

was always Blake that she'd wanted. 'I saw Amy when she was on *The Sharon Osbourne Show* back in October 2006,' said another friend. 'She had Blake with her. The entire time she was talking about "her boyfriend" – Alex – but was sitting on Blake's lap and snogging him. She was saying, "read me out those text messages I sent you – the filthy ones." It was all pretty gross. It was clear that they were still together. There's always been a kind of *Fatal Attraction* element to their relationship – it's like they can't live without each other.'

They certainly looked pretty happy together and the union had done nothing to dent Amy's popularity. ITV held a show in which viewers got to vote for Greatest Living Briton: while the Queen won the overall award, Amy beat such luminaries as Sir Elton John to come top in the music category.

Their friends were also full of the news. Plans were put in place to hold a sort of post-wedding hen night involving, of course, Kelly Osbourne, who was delighted for her friend. 'I had no idea they were gonna get married, none of us did,' she said as she planned to fly out to join them. 'Basically, Amy couldn't wait to share the news with me so she called me Saturday night and she was ecstatic. You know what Amy is like when it comes to her love of partying. She has planned a girls' only night, sort of like a post hen do. I'm so happy for her. Blake is a male version of her and I haven't seen her this happy before.'

And the low-key celebration was very much Amy's idea. 'I have spoken to Amy on the phone and she is so happy,' Kelly continued. 'Just looking at them together you can tell they are so in love. They are soulmates – anyone can see that. The wedding was a very small thing; Amy hates a lot of fuss. She would never do the whole big white dress, walking down the aisle with her dad thing.'

However, that self-same dad was not thrilled about the turn of events, not least because he would like to have been there. 'I'm not angry, just sad,' he said. 'I would have liked to walk her down the aisle.'

The controversy was briefly overlooked when Amy won her second Ivor Novello award for Best Contemporary Song for 'Rehab', making it her fifth award to date. 'Thank you all very much,' she said at the award ceremony back in London. 'I didn't even have time to get drunk, I've only been here about fifteen minutes.' Asked afterwards about the wedding, she said, 'It was all very sudden but that's the way I am. I had a lovely dress and he looked very hand-some. We're not planning a honeymoon. Every day is a honeymoon; I've married the best man in the world.'

'*Back To Black* was about my husband,' she said. 'The next one's going to be much happier. I'm going to write about Care Bears. My wedding ring doesn't fit me properly so I'm going to get it altered, then there'll be another ceremony for the family. My parents know what we're like. We did it for ourselves but we'll do all the other shit soon. I'm not the most eloquent when it comes to these [the Novello], but this award really means a lot. It's so prestigious and nice to be rewarded.'

But now she was back on British soil, the full weight of parental disapproval was beginning to weigh on her. Amy's mother and father were, after all, traditional Jewish parents, who had expected to see their daughter married with them present. Amy acknowledged as much. 'I'm going to have another bash – I've just got to,' she said. 'My dad is okay about it now, but I've got to do it again for him. This is the first time I've been home since the wedding, but I've married the best man in the world. We did it for ourselves. It was for us but we'll do another service for everyone else.'

In many ways, Amy was actually doing exactly what she always said she would. 'I'll be a Jewish wife, that's a promise,' she said before the wedding but added: 'I won't marry a Jewish man. I don't see that happening.' However, she did intend to run a traditional household. 'There are certain things that have nothing to do with religion, just to do with family and friends [being] at our house all the time,' she continued. 'It's all very social and about food.

That's the way Jewish families are. I will never stop cooking for them. I'd really like to get everyone in one place
and sit down and eat a meal together. I would like to up-
hold certain things, but not the religious side of things, just
the nice family things to do. At the end of the day, I'm a
Jewish girl.'

However, the rock 'n' roll lifestyle continued apace.
One of Amy's favoured regulars was the Hawley Arms in
Camden, north London, but after a night acting up, she
and her friends were banned. 'The manager and his staff
are at their wit's end with Amy and her pals,' said a source.
'Amy's hangers-on were throwing stuff out of the window
and being a nuisance. Eventually the manager ordered
them all out and Amy was told to sort it out or she wouldn't
ever be allowed back.'

The Shepherd's Bush dates finally took place, and Amy
got a rousing reception when they did. 'It's good to be
home,' she said. 'Thanks for giving me a chance after what
happened last time. I broke my tooth.'

She also took the opportunity to tease her parents, who
were in the audience. 'My dad's going to kick my arse later,
as he's still got to pay for the proper wedding,' she chortled.
'I got married to the best man in the entire world. That's
right, Dad, swallow that!'

And Elton John turned up, as planned: 'Amy is an

incredible performer,' he said. 'That was one of the most exciting and greatest shows I've seen in many years.'

In June, the line-up for the Glastonbury Festival was announced: Amy, needless to say, was among them. Shirley Bassey was another. But Amy remained adamant that this was not her entire life: 'I don't want to be ungrateful,' she said. 'I know I'm talented, but I wasn't put here to sing. I was put here to be a wife and a mum and look after my family. I've always been a homemaker. I love what I do but it's not where it begins and ends.' Of course, now that she was a married woman, the impetus to settle down was stronger – although that was not quite the way it turned out.

Meanwhile, plans were afoot for Amy and Lily Allen to duet at the MTV Video Music Awards in Las Vegas in September. 'Both girls have confirmed they'll appear,' said a source. 'Negotiations are now taking place with organisers who are eager to get the pair to collaborate on a duet for the show. Despite lots of hype, there is no bad blood between them and they have expressed a keen interest, meaning we'll have a massive moment in the show.'

In May, Amy's US success had become such that she made it on to the cover of *Rolling Stone* magazine. Underneath the headline, 'The Diva And Her Demons', the magazine pointed out that she had the most successful US debut of an overseas female artist, as well as talking to the people who worked with her, including Mark Ronson.

'Amy is bringing a rebellious rock and roll spirit back to popular music,' he said. 'Those groups from the Sixties like the Shangri-Las had that kind of attitude: young girls from Queens in motorcycle jackets. Amy looks fucking cool, and she's brutally honest in her songs. It's been so long since anybody in the pop world has come out and admitted their flaws, because everyone's trying so hard to project perfection. But Amy will say, like, "Yeah, I got drunk and fell down. So what?" She's not into self-infatuation and she doesn't chase fame. She's lucky that she's that good, because she doesn't have to.'

Amy herself was keen to talk about *Black to Back*. 'The songs literally did write themselves,' she said. 'All the songs are about the state of my relationship at the time with Blake. I had never felt the way I feel about him about anyone in my life. It was very cathartic, because I felt terrible about the way we treated each other. I thought we'd never see each other again. He laughs about it now. He's like, "What do you mean, you thought we'd never see each other again? We love each other. We've always loved each other." But I don't think it's funny. I wanted to die.'

As for the future, she maintained that having her own family was the most important thing. Asked if she would be upset if it all ended tomorrow, she replied, 'Not really. I've done a record I'm really proud of. And that's about it. It's just that I'm a caretaker and I want to enjoy myself and spend time with my husband. It doesn't even feel weird saying it now. Blake and I didn't get to spend any time together for a long while. And I was with someone else, and he was with someone else, and even six months ago I'd meet up with him and I remember saying to him so many times, "I just want to look after you."'

People continued to debate quite why Amy had been so successful. On the one hand, there was her undeniable talent, but on the other, she really was a breath of fresh air. For a start, she was so much more approachable than the vast majority of stars. 'For a while it was ridiculous,' one music writer explained. 'On any night, you could wander into the Hawley Arms and she'd be in there. So, you could have a drink with her if you wanted. If she wasn't in the Hawley, she'd always be around and about – I once saw her in Nando's ordering loads of chicken.'

This could bring problems in its wake, according to PR guru Mark Borkowski. 'Like many people of her generation, she's very comfortable with all the attention,' he said. 'There's a sense in which that whole circle – Pete Doherty, Kate Moss, et al – are anaesthetised to it. But there is a value to keeping yourself out of the press, because at some point, you may wish it to stop. That's going to be difficult for Amy Winehouse. She and her husband have sent out signals that they don't want to be left alone, and further down the line, I wouldn't be surprised if we saw her hand in the lens of some paparazzo.'

Amy certainly remained unconventional. Her in-laws still needed to have their own wedding celebration, and so Amy and Blake took his parents, Georgette and Giles, to the Mint Leaf Indian restaurant. They certainly weren't putting on any airs and graces: the restaurant, which was just outside Newark, Notts, had previously been a Little Chef by the A46.

'Mr and Mrs Civil have been regulars since we opened a year ago,' said the owner Babul Miah. 'They phoned and booked a table on Saturday evening, but we had no idea what it was for, or who their guests were until they arrived. I didn't recognise Amy until other guests got up and asked for her autograph. They told us it was a small family party to celebrate the wedding. They hadn't seen each other since Blake and Amy had arrived back from Miami.'

Babul's brother Saj, looked after the party while they were there. 'I put them on a large round table in the middle of the restaurant,' he said. 'When other customers started asking for Amy's autograph, Mrs Civil told them to leave her alone. She said that they were just out for a private meal to celebrate the wedding. But Amy didn't mind. She went out for a cigarette and signed autographs in the bar after she came back in. She was chatting to customers about her wedding and was very excited and happy.'

'They were all laughing and joking together. Amy and her mother-in-law were chatting together for ages. They seemed to have a lot to talk about. Blake and Amy were cuddling up and very affectionate with each other. It was a lovely family gathering. Mrs Civil did not want us to take pictures of them all together because it was a private party, but Amy was quite happy to pose for a picture with our chefs Amran Ahmed and Abdul Salam who cooked her meal. She said she really enjoyed it.'

'We've had celebrities in here occasionally but this is our first rock star,' said Babul. 'She seemed to enjoy a traditional Indian meal after the glamour of Miami.'

There was glamour of a different sort at the Glamour Women of the Year awards, at which Amy won UK Solo Artist of the Year, although she didn't actually turn up to the awards. However, there was also a sign that her famously volatile relationship with Blake had not been calmed down by marriage. At the MTV Movie Awards in Los Angeles, the two had a very public row.

'As soon as they walked into the lobby they started

screaming at each other,' said a witness to the scene. 'Amy was shouting: "You always fucking do this! Don't fucking touch me! Fuck you!" She was in tears but Blake tried to walk away. It wound her up so much she pushed him in a hedge. She calmed down a bit and walked over to Blake. Then she sat between his legs and they embraced. They were both crying and Blake said: "Why do you always fucking do this? I'm always propping you up." They were on the kerb for over an hour, sobbing and talking. They looked exhausted by the time they finally went to their room.' It might not have helped that her performance of 'Rehab' hadn't gone down very well.

There were further fears about the couple when they both appeared with fresh looking gashes on their arms. Amy had admitted self harming as a child, but seemed to have started again – as had Blake. Their co-dependency had become much darker, with both now encouraging each other to greater excess.

'Amy told me they egg each other on,' said a friend. 'She'd never admit to the hold Blake has over her. She does it to emulate him, to copy him, and that's dangerous. Privately she's said she cut herself because of work pressure. She's struggled with depression and says a blade piercing her skin makes her feel alive. She's worried fans and record company bosses will think she's a nutter – but it doesn't stop her. Once Amy cut herself with a broken champagne glass while touring America. That coincided with her seeing Blake again and he was self-harming too. Then she cut wildly at her tattoo of him as a sign that he was hurting her by cheating on her.

Amy even slashed herself when the two got back together. 'She slashed her arms with a razor,' said the friend. 'There was blood everywhere. That's what she did when they were back together!' It wasn't exactly a good omen of what was to come in the months ahead.

Rollercoaster

WHATEVER might have been going on in the background, Amy was still hitting the road. Mid-June saw her at the Isle of Wight Festival, in which she was a roaring success, living up to her reputation by first ordering twenty-four bottles of champagne in her hotel room and then participating in another drinking session in the Bacardi B-Live tent. Channel 4 attempted to interview her but stopped after a minute – all they were getting was monosyllabic answers. She did, however, demur when it came to taking one of the festival funfair's rides. Already strapped in, she suddenly changed her mind: 'She started screaming, "What about my hair – does it go upside down? Get me off!"' an onlooker reported.

There was also some hilarity at Amy's drinking habits. 'Amy was telling friends this weekend that she was on a "health kick",' said a friend. 'We were amazed, but then we realised that all this seemed to amount to was mixing fruit juice with her Bacardi instead of fizzy drinks. She was also saying that her drinks would be less calorific, although she hardly needs to be watching her weight.'

But a highlight came when the new kid on the block met pop royalty. The Rolling Stones were playing their first British festival for decades and at the end, Amy sauntered on to the stage. She and Mick Jagger then duetted to the Temptations number 'Ain't Too Proud To Beg', much to the joy of all the assembled fans.

But not everything ran smoothly. Kate Moss and Pete Doherty were present, and the former was reportedly rather irritated with Blake, who'd had too much to drink. 'Things were a tad tense earlier in the weekend because Amy's husband Blake Fielder-Civil was getting on her [Kate's] nerves, having drunk too much champers,' said an onlooker. 'He had been hassling Kate asking where Pete was, but he'd just nipped to the loo. So when Pete came back, Kate was quick to go off with her man and have fun, leaving Amy and Blake behind. But they are really good friends and enjoyed a giggle or two before Kate took her little girl onto the dodgems. Kate then went to meet Pete in the Bacardi B area before they went wild on other rides.'

Amy was also asked about the remarks she'd made a couple of weeks previously about wanting to be a mother. Rumours had been swirling that she was about to quit the music scene or at least take a break: Amy pooh-poohed the idea. 'Well, um, I am going to have a wicked summer; I can't wait to do all of the festivals. But I would love to have kids,' she said.

She certainly wasn't letting it all go to her head. Back on the mainland, she was spotted behind the bar at the Hawley Arms, pulling pints with the best of them. 'It helps pay the bills,' she said good-naturedly, when asked if she had a new job.

'Amy treated the pub like her own home, pouring herself vodka Red Bull drinks and choosing the music on the pub iPod,' said an observer. 'She poured shots and, pointing to a black sambuca, told punters, "This is on the house."'

And still the awards kept mounting up on the shelf. The latest was the Mojo Song of the Year Award: she arrived an hour and a half late and stuttered, 'I'm pretty shit at all this. Thank you, it's a real honour and I'm going to go and get drunk now.' This was crowned with a Mojo Woman of the Year. She had also been nominated for Best Album, but was (unusually) beaten by The Good, The Bad, and The Queen.

She got a bit of a taste of her own medicine at that stage, when she found herself on the receiving end of a drubbing from Cherry Ghost. It had been some years now since Amy had made a practice of lashing out at other musicians: she might well have been reminded of her past, however, when Cherry's front man Simon Aldred spoke out.

'I have been really trying at every stage to make sure I don't just have session players,' he said. 'Some of them play with amazing accuracy and professionalism but no real soul – they just collect the cheque at the end of the night. I think Amy Winehouse is brilliant, I think her songs are brilliant, but she doesn't know her fucking saxophonist from Adam, and that's not what it's about.'

Speculation that Amy was to sing the next Bond song heightened when David Arnold, who composed the three previous Bond scores, enthused about her talent. 'Amy Winehouse did the best record of last year,' he said. 'I haven't asked her yet, but I think she'd be good, although Bond songs can be a bit of a war zone. The next film will be in 2008, and we're almost finished with the script. The books are all done now so this one is going to be an extension of what happens to Bond, continuing the story on from *Casino Royale*. We haven't got a title yet, but anything without death, dying, tomorrow, or dies would be fine by me!'

Amy's next venture was Glastonbury towards the end of June. 'I don't care about the mud,' said Amy. 'It's Glastonbury, innit. You just get stuck in.' In the event, it was fortunate that that was her attitude: the rain poured on the 80,000 revellers, although one critic commented that the sun came out during one of Amy's songs. Her pre-concert request caused some amusement: two bottles of red wine, one large bottle of vodka, one bottle of champagne, one bottle of brandy, one case of lager, forty Marlboro Lights, chocolate, and three 'good quality' hot pizzas. The pizzas had to be hot because otherwise 'the band will refuse them', while 'two competent, sober local crew' was also asked for. On top of that: 'No sticky wristbands; access to and from the outside without going through the crowd; and please arrange parking as close to the load-in as possible.'

'This is the most boozy list organisers have received so far,' said an insider. 'They are talking to Pizza Hut about biking in the pizzas.'

Glastonbury was a washout – but only in terms of the weather. The festival itself was an enormous success, with Amy appearing alongside Arctic Monkeys, Kasabian, The Kooks, The Who, and numerous others – and she held her own. Indeed, she was appearing twice: at her Pyramid Stage show in the afternoon and again on the Jazz World stage in the evening. Drinking between acts was on the cards.

Still, it provided the opportunity for quality time with Blake. The couple rented a teepee at Camp Kerala, just outside the festival grounds, a luxurious place featuring tents with large double beds and in-room showers: the only fractious moment seemed to come when a girl nearby cast a glance at Blake. 'Leave my husband alone. He is married,' yelled Amy, dragging Blake back to the teepee: the pair disappeared for hours.

Her behaviour was certainly not calming down. In the middle of an interview, Amy slashed her stomach with a piece of glass to carve out Blake's name: fresh concerns surfaced that she might totally self-destruct. She herself said otherwise. On the eve of the Oxegen festival in Punchestown, Co Kildare, in Ireland, she reiterated that all she wanted was a domestic life of bliss: 'I've turned into a domestic goddess, honestly. I just want to be a happy housewife,' she said. 'That would be more than enough for me. There is something inside me that is a proper little housewife. I love cooking and doing the housework. Being married is the greatest gift ever. People will jump to conclusions that I have rushed into things because they see me as this mad person that the media portray. But I want a happy marriage like everyone else.'

As for criticisms that she was setting her younger fans a very bad example by cutting herself, she pulled no punches. 'I'm not in this to be a fucking role model,' she said. 'I don't care. I don't care about any of this, and I don't have much of an opinion of myself. I don't think people care about me. I made an album I'm very proud of and that's about it. I write songs because I'm fucked in the head and need to get something good out of something bad. I thought, "I'm going to die if I don't write down the way I feel. I'm going to do myself in". It's nothing spectacular.'

'All the songs I write are about human dynamics, whether it's with girlfriends, boyfriends, or family. When I did the last album, *Frank*, I was a very defensive, insecure person, so when I sang about men it was all like, "Fuck you. Who do you think you are?" The new album is more, "I will fight for you. I would do anything for you", or "It's such a shame we couldn't make it work". I feel like I'm not so teenage about relationships. I wouldn't say I'm a feminist, but I don't like girls pretending to be stupid because it's easier. People like to think I'm an out of control party girl, but it's not the case.'

Her record company bosses appeared to think otherwise. There was a fine line between raucous jazz diva and self-harming drunk, and Amy was teetering perilously close to the latter. She sparked real anger after pulling out of the Liverpool Summer Pops concert at the last minute citing exhaustion, and there were reports, denied by Amy, that her record company had set a twenty-four-hour minder on her. Certainly friends were concerned. 'Amy is teetering on the brink,' said one. 'Her drinking is wild. She has confessed to eating disorders and she has spoken in the past of her drugs hell.' She had been seen drinking in the Hawley Arms when she should have been in Liverpool; she then pulled out of T in the Park, again citing exhaustion. The world looked on, concerned.

There were also fears that her marriage wasn't doing her any good. Amy and Blake had a tempestuous relationship and many believed that the two of them drove each other to ever-greater extremes. Amy's father Mitch, as ever, was supportive. 'He's the perfect son-in-law,' he said. 'Blake is a traditional man. He asked me one night if I would mind if he asked Amy to marry him. I told him I didn't mind at all and to go for it. I liked him for what he did. It showed respect towards Amy and me. He's been very good to her and I was happy to welcome him into the family. Amy loves him and that's what's important. I've never seen her as happy as she is at the moment.' As for the rows: 'All this stuff about her and Blake arguing and not getting on is a load of rubbish. Honestly, when you see them together, they're like a pair of lovesick teenagers. They are so loving towards each other.'

Indeed, according to Mitch, parenthood beckoned. 'They are thinking of having children soon,' he said. 'She is all caught up in her career at the moment, but she often talks about wanting a baby. You just never know what she's going to do next. Amy will probably want to carry on writing and singing so I've told her I would help out with a baby. Her mum Janis and me can fight over who looks after him or her! I wouldn't want Amy to have a nanny; we'll give her all the help she needs. I can't wait to be a grandad, so hopefully Amy or her brother will let me be one soon. I've even joked that, when she has a baby, I'll kidnap it as I'll love it so much!'

And he remained extremely proud of his talented daughter, revealing that it was he, and not she, who kept hold of her growing number of awards. 'I keep all of them,' he said. 'I'm a typical dad and I love showing off what my daughter has achieved. I've got all the awards at home in the living room; they've taken over the mantelpiece. I'm going to find a room to put them all in. I'll probably need to open a museum if she carries on like this.'

But she clearly needed to pull herself together. Amy was by now pulling out of so many gigs that William Hill started offering odds of 1–2 that she would miss the next one, scheduled to take place in Cornwall at the Eden Project. She did actually make it on stage that night, but once there, worried onlookers again by her eccentric behaviour. 'Everyone thought Amy was acting rather strangely' said one. 'She was wobbling around the stage, muttering to herself, swearing, and slapping herself in the face. It was as though she was trying to snap herself out of something.' She also hit herself on the head with her microphone – the official announcement said that she was 'rusty' after being out of practice as a performer.

Even so, there was plenty to celebrate. The album *Back to Black* was nominated for a Mercury Award: she was immediately seen as one of the two main contenders, alongside Arctic Monkeys. She also played a gig at London's Somerset House: not only did she turn up, but she was even quite coherent. When there were a few boos at the end of her seventy-minute set (because of its brevity), she managed to laugh at herself. 'Boo you,' she said. 'I've been up here an hour and I haven't even collapsed yet.' Indeed, so well did it go that she announced an eleven-gig tour to take place in November. It was to prove a step too far.

Back then, at the height of the summer, the world was her oyster – when she made it on stage. She returned to the States, which continued to laud her, and got a greater accolade still when she appeared in an interview with American *Vogue*. Again, she revealed her domestic side. 'I'd love to have a beauty salon,' she said. 'My grandmother pretty much trained my brother. He'd give her a pedicure and I'd do her nails and hair.'

That was one week. Shortly afterwards, it all came crashing down again. Amy had been due to perform at the Oya music festival in Oslo, Norway, in early August: this time round, not only did she pull out on the day, but she was admitted to University College London Hospital suffering from 'severe exhaustion.' 'Amy Winehouse was admitted to UCLH this morning suffering from severe exhaustion,' said a spokesman for Island Records. 'Amy was discharged from the hospital this afternoon and has been advised to take complete rest. Scheduled performances in Norway and Denmark this week have been cancelled.'

Organisers of the Oya festival appeared to be distinctly unamused. 'The news of the cancellation came abruptly and surprisingly upon us a little before one o'clock this afternoon,' said an icy statement on the festival's website. 'Winehouse's large crew arrived yesterday, and her backing band had just finished their sound check when we were notified. So far no reason has been stated. We will be back with more news as soon as we have been informed.'

Of course, there were concerns that a good deal more than exhaustion might have been involved. Given Amy's increasingly erratic behaviour – and the fact that she was clearly using hard drugs – the real nature of what had happened was a matter of intense debate. 'Amy was at home in the early hours of Wednesday when she collapsed,' he said. 'Blake was desperately worried and had to get her to hospital. Everyone is really concerned. She has been hitting the bottle in an incredible way lately and lost so much weight. She has been cancelling gigs left, right, and centre, and it's not great for her professionally. She is having a tough time lately and has just cracked. The gigging, the drinking, that car-crash lifestyle... But with Amy, no one can tell her to look after herself. She's not the kind of person who listens. She is brilliantly talented and at the top of her game, but the pressure is immense. She can't help herself going into dark places. She needs a break from everything.'

Another put it more bleakly still. 'Amy is in a bad, bad way – and she knows it,' he said. 'This morning things looked dicey and it was A and E this time, not just a GP thing. A lot of us are really worried that her mind and body simply can't take the abuse. There's no point being the most talented person in the graveyard.'

Given the title of her most famous song, it was hardly surprising that the air was thick with calls for Amy to go into rehab, not least when details of what turned out to have been a three-day bender began to surface. 'It was like she had pressed the self-destruct button,' said a friend who was present. 'She was downing coke, pills, ketamine, vodka, and Jack Daniel's. Even Amy says she will be dead within one year. She had a party of people around before she collapsed. She looked like a zombie – white as a sheet and trembling. And I'll never forget her eyes. They were dead, like a shark's. At one point she strummed her pink guitar and sang and I thought, "Yes, the girl is back". But then she started rocking like a six-year-old and was wailing and sobbing.'

The party had started shortly after Amy's return from

the United States. She and Blake went to the Robert Inn in Hounslow, near Heathrow Airport, where she started knocking back vodka and lemonade, while Blake drank pints of beer. Lesley McCormack, a local at the pub, witnessed what happened next. 'Both Amy and Blake made repeated visits to the toilets during the two hours they were here,' she said. 'She went into both the ladies' and men's loos. They were with another woman. Amy ordered a club sandwich, asking for tuna instead of chicken – but she never ate it. She was a very nice person and signed some CDs for us and also had games of pool with the locals. It was surreal seeing them in there, as it really isn't the kind of pub that you see a rock and roll star in. There are normally only three old men in there.'

The revellers left after a couple of hours. Some time after that, they turned up at the Hawley Arms, where there were more witnesses as to what was going on. 'They were acting quite strangely,' said one. 'Amy was backwards and forwards to the toilets all night.'

The next day, Amy entered a café close to where they lived. 'She came in during the afternoon and was very jittery,' said the café owner. 'She wanted everything done now. She said she didn't know what she wanted but she said she wanted it hot. She was really out of it. I don't know what kind of drugs she was on. There was only one other customer, but we couldn't do it straight away. She said she needed hot food, but she couldn't wait. So I just sent her down the road to the pie shop and I saw her return within minutes with some pie and mash. I've only noticed her here in the last two months and she's normally very nice and comes straight in and goes straight out – but on Tuesday it was different.'

Hours later, Amy appeared to be going into convulsions, causing panic amongst Blake and her friends. 'Amy had boasted she hadn't slept in three days and her intake was taking its toll,' said one. 'Blake telephoned friends at 10pm, yelling "Fuck, fuck, she's having a fit!" The word went around like wildfire. Mates rushed around to help and Blake calmed down Amy by giving her water before taking her to hospital. He was terrified – but she was a mess. She didn't know what was going on.'

This time around it fell to Lance Fielder, Blake's father, to speak out for the pair, although he was honest about what was going on, too. 'Yes, she does work very hard,' he said. 'But exhaustion is a cover-up for a lot of other things. It was brought about by all her excesses. Work is one of them, but there's the drink and drugs, too. Blake told me he was very worried about her. He admitted they both drank and did drugs but that came as no surprise. She's got to get a grip on herself before it's too late. Amy is besotted with Blake. She's much happier when he's there and he wants to help her. Blake's a good influence on her. He's got a little bit more responsible since they've been together and he's trying to look after her. But Amy is a very strong personality and I wonder how much influence he can exert over her. There is only so much he can do.'

By now Amy had moved into a hotel, the Four Seasons at Hook, Hampshire, with Blake. The whole family, sick with worry, was getting involved. Mitch assembled a family gathering but to no avail: a scheduled trip to Germany was called off. 'I'm worried sick,' said Blake's mother Georgette Civil, who ran a hair salon in Newark, Notts. 'I don't know what's going on, but it's serious and I don't like it. I don't know if it's life threatening but, whatever it is, it's bad news. Amy and Blake are holed up in a room somewhere. We are all desperately worried. Mitch called and demanded we get together to try to knock some sense into Amy. I thought at first her problems were down to sheer exhaustion but now that's obviously not the case. Amy's holed up in a room with Blake. They won't talk to anyone, but hopefully they'll tell us what's been going on. We plan to spend two or three days together. He [Blake] just said, "Amy's bad". He sounded desperate. That's when I really started worrying because for him to ask for help means it is serious.'

She was clearly in a dreadful way. There was some speculation that she didn't want to go to rehab because, in the wake of the song, it would be too embarrassing. Mitch was said to have banned Amy from seeing Blake and urged her to tone down her touring commitments, though in truth he was as powerless to help as anyone else. Amy herself almost appeared to have given up: 'Amy has told her mum she is often suicidal and she knows she will die young,' said a family friend. 'Janis and the rest of the family persuaded Amy to go to the hotel to recover after her overdose. They hope that by getting her out of the scene around Camden she will be able to see what she is doing to herself. But Amy is determined that she will not go to rehab. She has no idea how close she came to dying. She has barely eaten anything and keeps being sick. She is in an incredibly fragile state, both physically and mentally.'

And Blake, for all his faults, seemed to be Amy's best chance for survival. 'Claims that she has gone to rehab are total rubbish,' said the friend. 'That's what her family desperately want her to do but she won't listen. The family went along with the record company when they first claimed she was suffering from exhaustion. But Amy is a lot more than exhausted – she needs help and she needs it fast. Her best friend, Juliette Ashby, had a massive go at her on Thursday night and Amy went mental – it's worrying when she won't even listen to her closest friend. Mitch believes the only person she will listen to is Blake – he said if Blake hadn't been awake, Amy would have died.'

It didn't help that the two sets of in-laws seemed to be blaming the other for their children's' problems, with reports of dreadful rows going on. 'Mitch has become increasingly angry that Blake's mum and dad don't seem to accept he has a problem,' said a friend. 'They blame everything on Amy. Mitch couldn't hold his tongue and leaned close to Blake's dad to tell him what he thought. That's when it all kicked off. Blake's dad started saying, "Get out of my face". He accused Mitch of trying to bully them. Then he started abusing Amy, saying some really nasty things. Mitch just flipped, got up, grabbed him by the throat, and wouldn't let go. It was total chaos. Everyone was shouting, trying to get them apart. Amy was there, looking very ill, and she was shouting at her dad, "Let him go. Get off him." It was unbelievable. You have to feel for Mitch. He's doing everything he can for his daughter. He wants her and Blake to get the treatment they need together, and thinks they need family support.'

And it must be said that Amy was far from innocent in all this herself. She continued to cultivate a friendship with Pete Doherty, much to the dismay of her family, while appearing to revel in her increasingly dissolute lifestyle. Nor was this anything new, although the scale of her drug taking had clearly increased. 'Amy's parents have known for years about her problems,' said a source close to the family.

'They never accepted them, but they hoped it was something she'd grow out of. What happened this week was the final straw. They needed to see her on their own terms to try to get their daughter back. They don't trust Blake to keep her free of drugs so they are watching her while she goes through a cold-turkey detox. She is already looking better, and talking it out with her dad has helped her focus on what's important and what she wants from life.'

When Amy herself was well enough to talk about what had happened, she appeared to be a little shell-shocked. 'It was just crazy – one of the most terrifying moments of my life,' she said. 'I don't know how to explain what happened. I don't really know myself. I can't remember what I looked like. I couldn't recognise myself. It was terrifying; I was terrified. I was so out of control. It just happened. It shocked me. I'm sorry – I just don't know what got into me. I never want to feel that way again. I've scared myself this time. I was all over the place. I know things have got to change. I have to sort myself out.'

That was an understatement. And not only was Amy putting her life at risk, she was also on the verge of ruining her chances in the United States. Up until then, the US adored her; Amy seemed to be one of the few UK entertainers who really could make it big over there. But a drugs overdose was not the right publicity for a rising star, and there were real concerns she might have blown it.

'It was the worst thing that could happen,' said a friend. 'She's been a bit of a headache for the record company for a while to be honest, due to her drink binges and confessions of self-harm. But this takes the biscuit. She's on the verge of establishing herself as a credible artist in the States, but this could be the nail in the coffin for that. Lily Allen had trouble with her visa recently over allegations she attacked a photographer. But drugs are a different kettle of fish. US Immigration won't be very welcoming at all and Amy needs her visa to go over there. But there's the very real possibility she'll have her visa taken off her and won't be allowed anywhere near. [In the past] she started turning up to interviews drunk and would keep drinking. We were worried she was going off the rails then – and the record company warned her that she'd have to go into rehab if it carried on.'

Mitch, of course, was completely beside himself. 'She is skinny as anything and dehydrated and looks like she has just come from a concentration camp,' he said. 'She is barely eating; she is not sleeping. I know that if she doesn't eat she is going to die.'

It really was a crisis point and, this time round, Amy pulled out of it. But it was far from being the end of her troubles. Indeed, the months ahead were to prove more turbulent still.

'Rehab Is A Cop-Out'

AS AMY BEGAN to recover, assuring fans that she was fine and was about to return to work, her in-laws continued to speak up in her defense. 'She is tired,' said Georgette Civil. 'It is the touring. It is non-stop. I believe Amy is suffering from stress and overwork. Touring, she doesn't sleep properly or eat properly. And yes, they do drink a lot, but so do a lot of other young people. Amy is like the girl next door. She goes down to the corner shop to buy food and chats to me in the kitchen about girlie things like fashion and clothes. She buys sweets for us and the boys, and has given me some lovely handbags.'

Amy herself was relying on her father. 'When I get self-destructive, I just need to spend time with my dad,' she said. 'Rehab is a cop-out.' Mitch, meanwhile, was keen to play down stories about what had gone on between the two families. 'I'm not going to say what happened with Blake's dad,' he maintained. 'This is a private family matter. Amy's will be fine. She knows she's been through a terrible ordeal and is now on the mend. We have been encouraged, after the initial scare, that she is now getting better and going to be all right.' Giles was rather less diplomatic. 'I don't want to discuss it. We believe in dignity and respect, unlike Amy's family,' he said.

Nor were the industry's worries calmed when Amy pulled out of yet another concert, this time supporting the Rolling Stones. The gig was taking place in Dusseldorf, Germany, but doctors were concerned that it was all going to be too much and ordered Amy to cancel her appearance. The Rolling Stones were in the dark quite as much as anyone else: 'She has just pulled out of the concert,' said a spokesman. 'That is all we know.'

Eventually, after a good deal of persuasion, the couple was persuaded to seek treatment in the United States. Meanwhile, Georgette revealed exactly what had really happened between the two families. 'You can't blame Amy and you can't blame Blake,' she began. 'They are both as bad as each other. It's the hardest thing in the world for me to say in public that my son and his wife have a drug problem. They've admitted it. It's not a crime to admit this and they must not feel ashamed.'

The admission finally came when the two were holed up in the Four Seasons. It had been patently obvious to everyone what was going on, but at least the pair felt they could now be open. However, after that confession, the two promptly had a relapse, and spent the night smoking heroin. It was after that that the families fell out. 'Mitch was very upset and angry,' said Georgette. 'Amy denied it to her dad, but later said she had taken heroin in her room with Blake. Mitch blamed Amy's husband and blew his top when Giles tried to defend him. Later Giles phoned him and he apologised unreservedly. Ironically, Mitch losing his temper at Giles has helped Amy and Blake.'

It certainly seemed to make them aware of the impact they were having on their families, and it was that which, for the first time, made them finally consider getting professional help. 'Both families are just very pleased and proud for them to recognise they have a problem and that they are making steps to cure it,' said Georgette. 'They couldn't have done it separately – it's something they had to do together. It's very reassuring to know they are getting the help they need. They're both lost but we are going to get them back. They have to take control of their lives.'

In the event, they didn't. Far from going to the United States, the pair briefly put in an appearance at the Causeway Centre, off the coast of Essex, before checking themselves out again and returning to London by helicopter. It was not quite the new start everyone wished for. 'We were praying they wouldn't bail out early,' said Giles. 'We don't want them to go back into their vicious cycle. Amy has had five days away from drugs and her self-esteem and confidence is slowly coming back. I hope she and Blake can take control of their lives.'

More concerts were cancelled, including Chelmsford's V Festival, although Amy kept saying she was all right. 'I wanted my mates to see that I'm okay and it's all cool,' she said. Blake, meanwhile, decided it was time to defend himself. 'Everyone thinks everything that what's happened to Amy is my fault and I'm the bad guy,' he said. 'But I just want everyone to know that I love Amy so much. She's so precious to me, she's my wife, and I want to take care of her, that's why I'm taking her back to rehab.'

Indeed, the two returned to the Causeway retreat, while Mitch said he was 'so very proud' of his daughter for confronting her demons. Both families 'are delighted Amy and Blake have decided to deal with their health issues,' he said in a statement, adding, 'I'd also like to sincerely thank Giles and Georgette for all their efforts and support.'

But all the parents remained dreadfully worried. 'I don't even think this is Amy's fault,' said her mother Janis. 'I think her brain's addled. This isn't Amy. It's as if her whole life's turned into a stage performance. A part of me has prepared for this over the years. She has said to me: "I don't think I'm going to survive that long". It's almost as though she's created her own ending. She's on a path of self-mutilation, quite literally. It's like a sickness, but she can't see it.'

Matters were not helped when a friend of Blake's claimed he held drug fuelled 'cutting' parties. 'He had loads of women, a whole harem of them,' he said. 'He just used to coast from one to the next. Amy became one of them. I saw those pictures of Amy's arms and you could see she had cut herself. I'm worried he will destroy her.'

He wasn't the only one. 'She would tell me about her "friend's" problems,' said Janis, who was now revealed to have multiple sclerosis. 'She sometimes said that one of them used to cut themselves, but I never realised then she might have been talking about herself.' As for the fact that Amy was finally in rehab, Janis added, 'It's hard and it hurts, but I know I can't help her right now. She's got to do that for herself and every day I can only hope she's strong enough to do it.'

Indeed, Amy appeared to be actively avoiding her mother. 'Sometimes I don't phone her because if I don't phone her, I don't get hurt,' she said. 'She can't just brush me off and say she's too busy or tired.' Indeed, she'd scarcely seen her since the wedding. 'She didn't want me to come round,' said Janis. 'She said she was tired. Blake was there. We said "hello", but I don't feel I can connect with Amy when he's around. It hurts, but I know I can't help her.

She's got to do that for herself and I can only hope she's strong enough.'

'To begin with, after she left home, she would ring me every day. Then, once she started travelling more, I started to feel a detachment. I think she was too young. She lacks the maturity to cope. For most of her life, I've been aware of needing to keep an eye on her. She's reckless. No one can stop her once she's made up her mind, but she never thinks of the consequences. Last summer she performed at a friend's wedding and was sick in the loos. Then, before Christmas, she admitted she had anorexia and bulimia. Her self-harming was never apparent. I've had twenty-three years of Amy having close escapes. As a toddler in her pram she once nearly choked on cellophane. Another time she went missing in the park. She's tough, like me – I see that as my gift to her.'

Despite all her problems, the music industry continued to adore Amy. In late August, she was nominated for four MOBO (Music of Black Origin) awards: Best UK Female, Best Song, Best International Act, and Best R&B. However, she was also forced to cancel her US tour on doctor's orders: 'Due to the rigours involved in touring, Amy has been advised to postpone her upcoming September US and Canadian tour dates,' said her publicist Tracy Miller. 'Her European and UK tour dates in October and November remain in place. Plans are being made to reschedule her US tour for early 2008. Until then, Amy has been ordered to rest and is working with medical professionals to address her health.'

She couldn't address the problems soon enough. On the night the MOBO nominations were announced, Amy and Blake sank to a new low: the pair booked into the Sanderson Hotel and emerged in the early hours of the morning sporting deep gashes. Both looked dreadful. 'It was a horrifying sight,' said an onlooker. 'Blake had all these deep scratches on his face and neck, like he had been attacked by a wildcat. They were still open and weeping and he winced at one point, so the injuries must have been painful. He'd obviously tried to stem the flow of blood with what looked like a T-shirt tied round his neck. But the attack marks went down to an angry-looking red patch and an open wound on his chest. It must have been a frenzied onslaught. And God knows what injuries he was covering up under his clothes.'

Amy was in an equally bad way. Her arms were bandaged, her feet and knees covered in blood, and her eye make-up had slid halfway down her face. 'It was the wildest she's ever been,' said the onlooker. 'She had a face like thunder and was clearly looking for trouble. Amy hit a few bars and was knocking back strawberry daiquiris like there was no tomorrow. Then she was wandering through the streets looking like a sad cross between a homeless child and a bag lady. She sprinted away and Blake chased after her, screaming her name like he was demented. But she didn't care. She flagged down a passerby and jumped in the car to escape.' Rehab evidently wasn't working.

Nor was this the only eyewitness account. 'Amy was running down street screeching like a wild animal,' said another observer. 'This guy in a hat was running after her screaming out her name, but she was moving so fast he couldn't keep up. Amy was covered in scratches and bandages and her clothes were covered in blood. She looked awful and was swearing at the top of her voice – she didn't care who heard her.'

A hotel worker, appalled by the state the two of them were in, rang the police, who turned up at the hotel at 5am. 'They looked a complete mess, as if they'd been in a massive fight,' said a witness to the scene. 'Amy was bandaged up and blood was dripping everywhere. She was totally zombified. Blake's wounds were horrendous too.' Mitch was again alerted and came to the scene: 'Obviously I am concerned, but Amy is with Blake,' he said wearily, in the aftermath. 'She's okay.'

But she clearly wasn't. Amy's own explanation, while bizarre, put the whole episode in an even worse light: the fight began, he said, when Blake attempted to stop her from taking drugs with a prostitute. 'Blake is the best man in the world,' she said. 'We would never ever harm each other. I was cutting myself after he found me in our room about to do drugs with a call girl and he rightly said I wasn't good enough for him. I lost it and he saved my life. I'll be all right. I need to fight my man's corner, though. For the last time, he did not and never has hurt me. He has such a hard time and he is so supportive. He deserves the truth. He is an amazing man who saved my life again and got cut badly for his troubles. All he gets is horrible stories printed about him and he just keeps quiet, but this is too much.'

Like Amy, Giles was keen to defend his son against accusations of violence. 'They've fallen out and Amy's gone a bit frenzied,' he said. 'She's got her claws into his face. Blake's a dignified person. He wouldn't hurt Amy – not even in self-defence. But clearly she's gone hell for leather. It's nasty. The trouble is Amy, does like to have her own way and she can be quite willful. What Amy wants, Amy gets. But Blake hasn't been supplying Amy with drugs. There are people close to her who do. I've named one of them to the Metropolitan police and they're now investigating. These dealers are playing with people's lives here. What you've got is these two idiots, Amy and Blake, allowing themselves to be manipulated and controlled by a whole host of people with an incredible vested interest.'

Giles was also keen to make the point that Amy had been taking drugs long before she met Blake. 'Amy's dad Mitch said she was dabbling in drugs at thirteen,' he said. 'This is a girl who's had an eating disorder for a long time. These aren't new problems. It's totally unfair to blame Blake. He was a very kind, intelligent boy who dreamed of becoming a journalist. I never thought he'd end up like this.'

'We know Amy and Blake are both into self-harming. Amy has a longer history of it, but this a new thing for us. Blake never did it at home. We've seen cuts on his arm and asked about it, but he just sort of waved it away. He can be very vague when he wants to be. 'It's a psychological problem – people do it when they don't feel in control. It's their way of getting back in charge. But with the two of them self-harming it's very worrying.'

Mitch, of course, had been terribly upset by pictures of the two of them covered in bandages and blood – given that her ballet shoes were also blood-stained, there was some speculation that Amy had been injecting heroin between her toes. 'It was sickening seeing those pictures. No, it was worse than sickening – I wanted to die,' he said. 'Those pictures made me see that here were two people completely out of control.'

They were indeed. Giles, however, was adamant that it was Amy's decision to leave the Causeway clinic, and that Blake had wanted them to stay. 'My son didn't want to come out,' he said. 'But if Amy's insistent, he wants to support her. I offered for them to stay with us for a bit. It would have been quite peaceful for them. But they said they were going into London – to get back to normal. It makes you wonder how much they need that lifestyle. As I drove home, Blake phoned me to say they were in a hotel. I spoke to both of them and they came over very happy, calm, and relaxed. The next thing I hear is Blake's pictured in the street with Amy at 3am and covered in scratches. It's all a bit of a shock. Blake's an intelligent boy, but he clearly doesn't use his head sometimes.'

'I don't think having a break from each other is the solution. It sends out the wrong signals. I think they need professional counselling. But we can't drag the horses to the water, let alone make them drink it. There's so little I can do. The little advice I do give them they'll plainly ignore. I won't dictate and try to manipulate them. I can only be there for them if the need arises. But clearly this doesn't paint a good picture of their relationship and that's a shame. If it seems appropriate that the marriage should dissolve, then so be it.'

And, of course, Amy also had her say. 'Look at me, I'm

a mess,' she said to one paper. 'I'm nothing special. In fact, I'm nothing at all. I don't feel good. I don't have talent. I'm nothing without my husband. I love him so much sometimes it hurts. I owe him everything. Without him I would be nothing, which is why it is so important we are together right now. I can't beat the drugs without him. He's my rock, and as a married couple we need to go through everything together. Blake says he isn't going back to rehab – but I can if I want. But I'm not going without him.'

If truth be told, Amy was now so dependent on Blake, she seemed to lose any kind of clear view as to who she actually was. Blake had nothing to do with her talent and success (other than inspiring *Back to Black*) and yet Amy was now behaving as if only he could keep her going at all. 'I know I need help, but Blake's the only one who can help me,' she said. 'I don't want to lose him. I won't lose him. I want to make him happy – like what he does to me. I feel disgusting and Blake's the only one who stops me feeling like this. I'm not talented. I don't feel very amazing. I feel flattered you'd say that, but I know it's not true. I'm useless and just keep messing up. I'm lucky I've got a caring husband – I don't deserve him. I can't believe he even wants to be with me. I don't understand why. All I know is that I'm the luckiest girl alive to have someone as caring as Blake.'

It was looking very much as if she was now addicted to

Blake as well as to everything else. The Sanderson, unsurprisingly, took rather a dim view of the proceedings and
asked them to leave, at which point they checked into the
Covent Garden hotel. Matters weren't much better there.
'Amy and Blake yo-yoed from their room to the hotel bar
every five minutes,' snapped on of their fellow guests. 'At
one point Blake raced up to their room and locked Amy
out while she banged on the door for five minutes, calling:
"Baby, let me in. Baby, are you all right, are you all right?
Let me in!" before he opened the door. She also kept going into the men's toilets which we thought was a bit odd.'
Later on, Blake caused more upset when he and a friend
raced down the corridors banging on people's doors. They
left very early the next day.

And so, as was now becoming the norm, both sets of
parents publicly intervened. Giles Fielder-Civil risked
angering not only Amy, but also her family, record company, and fans, when he went on Radio 5 Live and, on the
Victoria Derbyshire programme, suggested people should
stop buying Amy's records. 'Why don't the record company
do more?' he asked. 'We believe that the record company
should be proactive in helping the couple get better. At the
moment they seem to be hiding behind a label that the pair
aren't drug addicts, they're exhausted or whatever.'

'The pair have gone on holiday. That isn't helping them.

It's just getting them out of the way. We urge the record company to do something. There are a lot of people that surround the couple who do have a vested interest. We have tried to contact the record company again but we have received no reply. It's about time that their friends and their professional colleagues say to them "enough is enough". Perhaps it's time to stop buying records. It's a possibility. By doing that, it affects the record company, and the record company may take notice.' If that were not enough, he then called on the record company to suspend Amy's contract, before suggesting they were close to death: 'They're very close to the edge and if one of them dies through substance abuse, the other will probably commit suicide,' he said.

An incensed Mitch then rang in, to say that the record company, the management company, and, indeed, every-one else, had been doing all they could. Indeed, a meeting had been arranged between drug specialists and everyone else to see what could be done. 'Unfortunately Giles and Georgette were due to come to that meeting. They came down to London. But instead of coming to that meeting to sit with the doctors and representatives of the record company and me, they chose to go to the pub with Amy and Blake. This is the problem we find ourselves up against. We have two families pulling in different directions. Basically we just want the same things, we want our children to be safe. But we've got different definitions of how we can do that. Had they also been in that meeting, some of the accusations they've made about the record company, about trying to work them to the bone and things like that, they would have heard me telling the record company that all of Amy's functions, certainly for the next three months, were cancelled on the spot.'

'There's no question of the record company or her family trying to work her to the bone. These are some of the accusations that have been levelled at us. They will have seen caring, loving people from the record company, people who have been in the business for twenty or thirty years who are used to seeing matters like this, crying their eyes out because of their genuine love and affection for Amy. The record company isn't as callous as some people think it is. There's only one person to blame and that's Amy. That's what Blake's parents have got to understand. It's no good blaming anybody else. This is Blake's fault and Amy's fault.'

'There are some extremely serious problems in their relationship,' he said. 'One minute they are covered in blood and a few hours later they are walking arm in arm. I have tried forcing Amy to do things and it doesn't work. So the doctors told me to try gently and make them think they were taking control. But that didn't work either. The only way is for Amy and Blake to take control. The only way out of this is not sectioning them, not locking them up. The only way out is for them to reach rock bottom, which I hope they already have. Then they will realise they don't want to do this any more and they have people who love them.'

As all the chaos raged back in London, Amy and Blake had rushed to St Lucia in the Caribbean for a holiday. There, initially, they gave every appearance of being a young couple in love: very briefly, their lives appeared to calm down. 'I texted her to see if she was okay, and she replied saying she was right as rain and she said, "I love you, dad",' said Mitch.

Inevitably, it didn't last long. Amy stripped down to her bikini, revealing not only more scars from cuts, but also what looked very much like marks from where she'd been injecting drugs. Both sets of parents leapt straight in. 'When Amy showed us her body there were no suspicious marks in the joint of her elbow,' said Giles. 'There was no bruising of any kind. They've been in St Lucia for around six days, since Sunday, and this kind of bruising is maybe two or three days old, I guess, I don't know. If you want to avoid drugs, you don't go to the Caribbean. I would imagine the dealers of St Lucia thought, "Great, we're going to eat for a month now." Last month Blake and Amy showed us they don't inject, and we believed that. I believe they've got a drug problem. If they are injecting they are just on the road to hell.'

Matters were now clearly spiralling totally out of control. Mitch was right: Amy and Blake were locked into a totally self-destructive cycle, egging on each other to further drugs and cutting, destroying each other as fast as they were destroying themselves. It was also badly damaging Amy's career: she was no longer favourite to win the Mercury prize and her cancelled US tour meant she had almost certainly lost American sales. But still this was not rock bottom. Worse was yet to come.

What Planet
Are You On?

THE MERCURY AWARDS came and went: as forecast, Amy lost out. The winners of the £20,000 prize were the Klaxons. But at least she turned up: it was her first public appearance since the dramas of the previous week, and she even performed one song to rapturous applause, while spending the rest of the evening draped around Blake. 'She was very happy to be here,' said the ever-loyal Mitch. 'And I'm just thrilled she was here. She gave a brilliant performance and she looks well.'

The host of the evening, Jools Holland, was equally effusive. 'She had one of the best voices of anybody of all time,' he said.

There was a great deal of support for the troubled star. Lily Allen, her erstwhile rival, had already sent a card and flowers, and at the GQ Men of the Year awards, where she was presenting the best band award to the Kaiser Chiefs, she again offered her good wishes. 'My heart goes out to her. I feel for her so much with everything that's happened and I really hope she's okay. You don't need drugs to be creative. No one needs them. I have my problems but they are nothing compared to Amy's. It can't be very easy for her to deal with her demons in the spotlight. I can't imagine how hard it is for her.'

Amy herself appeared determined to pull herself together. The Sid and Nancy warning had hit home: she vowed publicly the couple would not end up the same way. Indeed, there was much comment about how much better she was looking after her short break. But one person who was not even remotely reassured was Janis, who revealed that she sent Amy text messages asking, 'What planet are you on? Call me.'

She was clearly very worried. 'Amy is playing Russian roulette with her health and musical gift,' she continued. 'She's lost herself. We're not talking about my Amy. It's not someone I recognise. She has become her own stage creation. I knew she was smoking marijuana but not that she was doing Class A drugs until she collapsed. She won't stop until she sees the point of stopping. When I saw her afterwards, I did not tell her to clean up, there was no point. I know all about Class A drugs. I understand the process where the brain shuts out everything except the drugs. Talking to her about it won't make any difference.'

Amy's personal issues were causing other problems, too. Until the autumn of 2007, she had been seen as almost the dead cert as the voice of the next Bond film, but now doubts were voiced about this, too. 'A month ago Amy was thought to be a shoo-in for the theme tune to Bond 22,' said a source at the film production company EON. 'Her voice and musical style was in perfect sync with what Bond is all about. There was even talk of her having a cameo by performing the theme tune in a smoky club Bond visits – but that's out of the window now. After all the reports of hard drug use, self-injury, and domestic violence, it's fair to say the bosses here just aren't keen on the idea.'

And her situation was beginning to attract comment from very established members of the music industry. Annie Lennox was one person who voiced concern, both at the fascination with Amy and her male counterpart, Pete Doherty. 'It's what you call the "life crash chic",' she wrote on her Internet blog. 'You know when there's been some kind of accident, how the cars slow down while everybody rubbernecks the scene? Well it's like that, but in slow motion. And the crash victims seem to be "successful" young women who have become high profile for one reason or another, yet have somehow become derailed.'

'They make damn good drama. Living soaps. And as long as we are fascinated by the details of the crash, the culture will continue on its long dark course … it needs consumers, followers, voyeurs, to re-create itself. So I see the covers of a plethora of magazines, and skim through the inner contents. The "shock horror" of recurring rehab, domestic abuse, self abuse, weight gain, weight loss, break ups, make ups, new hair style ... tits in, tits out, new designer shoe ... whatever.'

George Michael, himself no stranger to drug use, was another who voiced his concern. 'This is the best female vocalist I have heard in my entire career and one of the best writers,' he said on 'Desert Island Discs'. 'All I can say is, "Please understand how brilliant you are." We must support her.'

The Scottish singer KT Tunstall, who, like Amy, had had very quick success and who, like Amy, had started drinking too much to deal with it, was also kind. 'Amy finds the fame side difficult and alcohol is obviously a way of dealing with it,' she said. 'During my first year of being famous, alcohol was a way of chilling out and escaping from the total madness that can ensue when you have success.' She had, however, been a little older – twenty-nine. 'I'm sure I would have been a total mess if I was her age,' she said.

'I don't want to be in the newspapers looking wasted, falling over, and being sick on stage. It's just not my thing. I've never behaved like that, so if I want to get hammered in a nightclub, I'll make sure I don't tell anyone. From my experience, there's a choice to be made whether you have that kind of attention or not. If that's what Amy wants, then it comes with its demons.'

However, there were rumours in the industry that Amy's record company was beginning to get seriously cheesed off. They had had great hopes for their new star, but her behaviour had probably lost her the Mercury award, the next Bond theme tune and, worst of all, she was playing very badly in the United States, where she had been expected to make great headway. No one from Island Records would talk publicly, but industry insiders were prepared to lay it on the line. Amy and her male counterpart, Pete Doherty, were beginning to cause serious dismay.

'If they want to fuck themselves up on heroin,' said one, 'they could do it at a house in the middle of the country. But they don't. They do it before running around the streets of Soho. This idea that all publicity is good publicity is not true. There comes a point when you cross a line and staggering around the streets with blood on your face is not good publicity.'

'I think a lot of people now wish Pete Doherty would just get banged up, fuck off, and shut up, and I fear that some people will start thinking that about Amy, too. As regards the record company: there is a lot of personal contact and feeling, but there's only so much a company can do to help when people show no sign of wanting to help themselves, and even their families and friends seem to have no influence. How can it be in Island's interests to have Amy dead when the company is hoping for five more platinum albums?'

Amy turned twenty-four on 14 September – Blake bought her a vintage jukebox – and celebrated at a party at the London members' club Century. 'I didn't enjoy re-hab,' she told a journalist present. 'I don't want to go back. I missed my friends and my mum and dad. They are the ones who are there for me. I have been doing better now and that's because of my friends. I'm drinking tonight and I'm enjoying myself. It is my birthday. But drugs are private. Let's just say, I feel better than I felt ever before. Blake is the best husband in the world. He organised this party. It's the best present in the world.'

Indeed, she was keen to play down her recent travails, as well as pouring scorn on rumours doing the rounds that she and Blake were trying for a baby. 'I'm sorted out,' she said. 'Nothing's wrong with me. I'm writing some new stuff and can't wait to be back on tour. Babies? Not yet, not yet! It's not my priority. But I would like to have children one day. I'm just concentrating on work now.'

As for the recent holiday: 'It was a honeymoon and I am so happy,' she said. 'I am ecstatic. I am elated. We are just married and we don't need anybody else. We are so much in love. A lot of fuss has been made about nothing. There's nothing wrong with me. In fact, I feel better than I've ever felt before.'

Unfortunately, her behaviour didn't reflect this. There had been intense speculation as to whether she would turn up to the MOBO Awards, at which she was scheduled to sing: she did, and won Best Female, but put on a shambolic performance that had onlookers gawping in dismay. She forgot many of the words of 'Tears Dry On Their Own', before putting on a marginally better performance of 'Me And Mr Jones', but it was clear all was not well. 'In her dressing room she was really on edge, then flipped,' said a source. 'She was screaming and chucking anything she could get her hands on at the people around her. She wasn't in a good way.'

But people continued to stand up for her. There had been a great deal of grumbling that she wasn't a good role model for young women: the veteran singer Paul Weller took issue with that. 'She is a great role model,' he said. 'I don't think the drugs and the drink make a scrap of difference. You should judge people on their talent and on that level she's up there, a major talent.' The music industry certainly agreed, naming her Best Live Female at the Vodaphone Live Awards.

There were also hopes – soon to be dashed – that Amy's

birthday party had made her reassess her relationship with Blake. 'Amy's party was a watershed,' said a friend. 'At the start of her relationship with Blake everyone liked him. Then they saw another side but tolerated him and thought that he still had her best interests at heart.'

'But after his reaction to her overdose everyone agreed enough was enough – and ignored him at her birthday. He was at one side of the room with a few mates; Amy's pals were on the other. She's now confronted him and he admitted that after her overdose, he left her, out of it in her hospital bed, to go and take more drugs. Now Amy's mates think she may have seen light at the end of the tunnel. A relationship this intense and explosive just can't last. This could be the beginning of the end – fingers crossed.' It proved to be anything but.

Certainly, there was no shortage of people prepared to stand up and talk about what a disastrous influence Blake was. 'Blake was off the scene, she had another boyfriend,' said one assistant, who had worked with her on *Back to Black*. 'She has enormous talent and deep roots in jazz and blues; she didn't suffer from the "lead singer syndrome" and unlike most she knew her sharps and flats. And she knew exactly who she was and how she wanted to sound – which some singers only know when they've got forty grand's worth of equipment, but which Amy knew by standing on top of a piano in a pub. I want people to know that Amy is not the idiot they think she is from the papers. She drank too much. But at twenty-three that doesn't make you an alcoholic, and everyone on the road drinks too much. I've been around a few junkies, but I never saw any sign of that until Blake came back. He was introduced as the ex-boyfriend; the coke started arriving, and he had those rings round his eyes – as I said, I've known enough junkies.'

'He stuck to her like glue and they soon became inseparable. I think Amy's wonderful and that's the tragedy – think Billie Holiday, Edith Piaf, and her favourite, Dinah Washington. The worst thing is that she knows what she is doing. You can't tell her anything about what she is doing that she doesn't already know.'

Matters rapidly degenerated. After spending an admittedly short time keeping it together, Amy lost it again, this time by illegally leaping over the Eurostar barrier in London's Waterloo train station when she was on her way to Paris. The problem seemed to be the absence of Blake: Amy had bid him farewell earlier in the day and now seemed to have a sudden change of mind. 'Amy was crying, gesticulating wildly, and shouting while the man with her was trying to calm her and get her through the gate,' said a fellow passenger.

'She mentioned Blake's name more than once.

Eventually they went through security, but then Amy came running back. She hurdled the security gate then ran up the escalator, shouting and screaming, into Waterloo station concourse. It was quite a sight – this tiny girl with a massive beehive leaping over a barrier. It was pretty clear she was not keen on getting on that train to Paris.' The police were forced to intervene and eventually persuaded her to get on the train.

Nor was it auspicious when she changed some of her tour dates from November to December. Fans and supporters were clearly desperate to see her out at her best, performing again, but for those in the know, clearly all was not well.

But she tottered on. In October, *Back to Black* won best album at the Q Awards, although she didn't actually turn up to receive it – just as well, perhaps, as the host, Jonathon Ross, made some very close-to-the-bone jokes at her expense. Mark Ronson picked it up on her behalf and promptly left it in the toilets of a Soho nightclub where, fortunately, it was rescued by the cleaners: 'Mark Ronson came in carrying the award, but when he left at 12.30am he didn't have it,' said a spokesman for Bar Soho. 'The cleaners found it in the male toilets this morning. Neither Mark nor his management have contacted us about the award.'

Mark was beginning to think about her new recording.

Showing off his-and-hers tattoos of each other's
names, Blake and Amy appear loved-up and happy at
the MTV Awards in June 2007.

Blake and Amy pose outside The Brewery in London at
the Mojo Awards, June 2007.

(*Above*) – A noticeably thinner Amy performs at the Vodafone Summer Series at Somerset House in London, July 2007.

(*Left*) The newlyweds enjoy a day out shopping in New York. The signs of Amy's eating disorders are all too clear.

Amy and Blake take a break from shopping in
New York to steal a kiss.

A gaunt and emaciated Amy walks the streets of
New York, August 2007.

Amy and Blake strolling through Covent Garden
the morning after their very public row. The cuts and
scratches on Amy's arm and Blake's face are
all too obvious.

Amy, escorted by her father Mitch, on the way to
Blake's court hearing.

Her trademark beehive gone, a blonde and bony Amy
walks the streets of London with her father Mitch, in
January 2008. The beehive would return in
a matter of weeks.

Amy's schedule was still hectic, but a new record was in the pipeline, and it was time to see in which direction it should be heading. 'I'd really like to make it sound older or more morbid or really "Wall Of Sound",' said Mark. 'But I don't want to second guess before I actually hear the songs.'

Behind the scenes, though, nothing had calmed down. Mitch continued to be as worried as ever, even confessing that he'd written a speech to be read at Amy's funeral, should such a thing be required. 'I wrote a eulogy for Amy myself last month,' he said. 'When she had her seizure and was taken to hospital, I really thought that could be it. The doctors told us even a whiff of another drug could kill her.'

Nor was there any easing in the war of words between the two families, with Mitch publicly blaming Blake for Amy's problems. 'It was as bad as someone holding a gun to my daughter's head. Blake is a bad influence on her and I no longer toe the line and pretend he isn't. Amy is responsible for her own actions but, until he came along, she was staunchly against hard drugs. For Amy and Blake to beat their drug problems they have to go into rehab separately and he won't let her do that. I don't care about his health at all, except that my Amy's happiness depends on it. In the end, she's my daughter. She's very strong and I love her. I trust she will be all right.'

Another person whose company Amy was keeping was

Pete Doherty, possibly the only person in Britain whose behaviour rivalled her own. There was even talk of the pair working together, and they managed to sober up for long enough to record something. 'It's a ska-type track,' said guitarist Mick Whitnall. 'Amy's playing guitar on it, and singing as well. She plays better than James Brown playing acoustic guitar. She thinks she's shit but she's not. I've never met a man who plays like that, let alone a girl.'

Amy kicked off her autumn tour with an appearance in Berlin, but it didn't take long for trouble to rear its head. The next stop was Norway, where she, Blake, and a friend, Alex Foden, were arrested for possession of drugs. They were held overnight in the police cells and she was fined €500 (£350), although she still planned to take to the stage. 'She was released without charge this morning,' said her spokesman Shane O'Neill. 'The show in Bergen is going ahead as planned.'

'They are very strict about drug taking in Norway,' said a witness. 'With her past record they thought there was more than just a couple of spliffs. When she opened the hotel room door it was obvious she was wasted. She was mumbling and no one could understand her. Amy and Blake were put in separate cells but Amy couldn't be interviewed straight away because she was totally incoherent.'

Such was the state Amy had got herself into by that

time that there was actually a good deal of relief back home when it was revealed that the drug in question was marijuana. It could have been a great deal worse. 'We were chuffed when she was caught with cannabis,' said a friend. 'Everyone used to worry about her cannabis habit, but now we look back at those days fondly. We have been telling her to quit the hard stuff and get back on the weed.'

The Norwegian authorities were actually pretty good about it. 'We had a tip from a good source which led to police checking up on the tip,' said prosecutor Lars Morten Lothe. 'They were in a hotel room in the centre of Bergen. She signed a ticket – a fine – at the police station some hours ago. It is a closed case.'

It might have been in Norway, but there were renewed fears Amy was jeopardising her chances of success in the United States. With not only her reputation, but also now a drugs charge behind her, it was looking increasingly difficult for her to get a visa to perform. Her management was in despair. 'Her management has been keeping a close eye on both her and Blake to try to ensure it was a trouble-free tour,' said a source 'The pair of them have mostly been holed up in their tour bus. But after Wednesday night's gig in Copenhagen, her manager flew back to London and it's since then that the trouble started.' Amy herself was keen to do more in America: 'I just love the States,' she said. 'I will definitely have a crack at America again. I want to be back there later this year.'

In the short term, she managed to put her woes behind her, moving on to Copenhagen, and even fitting in some sightseeing while she was there. She also showed herself to have at least some perspective on what was going on. Amy might have been wasted half the time, but she was fully aware of what she was doing. A DVD was being made called *I Told You I Was Trouble*, and in it she tried to analyse what her life had become. 'I was just doing one destructive thing after the other,' she said. 'I was quite self-destructive. Life's short – just do it. Do you know what I mean? Life's short and I've made a lot of mistakes, you know.'

'I always say I don't regret things and I don't say sorry, but I do really. I believe strongly in fate. I believe that every-thing happens for a reason. I'm quite an insecure person. I'm very insecure about the way I look. I mean, I'm a musi-cian; I'm not a model. The more insecure I felt, the more I'd drink. And to Tracey Trash, who does my hair, I'd be like, "Bigger! Bigger!" – like the more insecure I feel, the bigger my hair has to be. I didn't really think it was extraor-dinary to sing. I thought everybody could sing. I thought I'd be a waitress or something, or a housewife.'

Back on tour, she seemed to be resolving to clean up her act, saying that she wouldn't drink before her shows.

'This tour started pretty much as the last one ended,' said a source. 'Berlin was a difficult time for everyone and we thought it was going to turn into another tour full of drunken and missed shows. But she's now said that she will not drink before her gigs for the rest of the tour. She stuck to it in Amsterdam, amazingly, and gave her best show of the tour yet. Everyone just hopes she keeps it up.'

Willem Luyken, who organised the Amsterdam concert, confirmed this. 'She wasn't drunk when she came in and she did not drink backstage,' he said. 'I don't think she was stoned either. People were joking about her sober performance. They said, "Has the wine bar been closed today?" But no, she was sober until after her performance. She said she won't drink before shows any more – only afterwards.' Unfortunately, she was not to keep that up.

'I really thought I was on the way out,' she said in an interview with Germany's *Stern* Magazine. 'Blake saved my life, brought me into the hospital. Often I don't know what I do. Then the next day the memory returns. Then I'm engulfed in shame. Recently I saw a picture of myself when I came out of the hospital. I didn't recognise myself. Since I was sixteen, I have felt that a black cloud hangs over me. I have taken pills for depression. But they slowed me down. I believe there are lots of people who have these mood changes. I just have this good luck to have found this outlet in my music. I believe I live through pain. If you suffer for something it means to me that it is not unimportant.'

It was a fine way to look at it, but Amy's family and friends remained terrified of what she might do next. She was clearly still extremely fragile, and her relationship with Blake seemed to make that even worse. She constantly told people she had no talent, which might have displayed a fine lack of pop star ego, but indicated an insecurity that was out of control, and it seemed to take just the slightest thing to tip her over the edge. And so, alas, it was to prove. Amy was getting close to the start date of the UK leg of her tour, something that was to highlight her problems more starkly than anything yet. She was also about to be involuntarily separated from Blake, which seemed to send her closer to the edge than ever. Friends were beside themselves – such talent and yet she risked throwing it all away. It was heart-breaking – but ultimately the only person who was going to be capable of helping her was Amy herself.

Meltdown

AMY'S LIFE WAS by this time a soap opera with a very dark edge. Everything she did was under surveillance, everything was commented upon. But it was a measure of the affection in which the industry held her that older, more experienced stars constantly expressed their concerns for her and their worries that she could throw it all away.

Simon le Bon, frontman of Duran Duran, spoke out. 'We didn't want to get banned from America, so we were careful,' he said. 'No one saw us publicly get up to any mischief but I can assure you we did and we were pretty wild. There was apparently a hotel in LA where you could order drugs on room service but we never found it. But I worry today that Amy Winehouse could kill her career if she's not careful. Any kind of drug conviction can get you banned from America, and Amy has the potential to be massive over there. This is her time, her moment, and I'd hate to see her waste it.'

Mitch, unsurprisingly, felt the same way. He was again

doing a publicity blitz across the media in an attempt to shake Amy out of it, and now went on ITV's *This Morning*. And he was adamant that matters changed when Blake came on the scene. 'It's apparent in her music that she's smoked dope for quite a while, probably from the age of sixteen or seventeen, perhaps even earlier,' he said. 'She was a complete opponent of hard drugs – in fact, she got up and said she couldn't understand why people in the music industry took hard drugs and that changed about six months ago when she got married to Blake.'

'And I'm not saying it's Blake's fault, what I'm saying is Amy's responsible for her own actions. However, it's a fact that the hard drugs coincided with their marriage. She's not drinking as heavily as she was then, actually, but there are other problems. The other problem is the bulimia, which is still apparent; although she's put on about a stone in weight, it's still affecting her health. And there are problems with substance abuse as well. But it's not as bad as has been reported.'

Naturally, however, he was desperately concerned about the longer term. 'We do think, where is it going to end up?' he said. 'And we don't know. But as I've said before, at the moment she decides that enough is enough, all the help she needs will be in place. Her family is there, the doctors are there, and the facilities are there should she wish to make use of them. We're not completely helpless; things are in position.

And he was strongly defensive of Amy, although he did say that he now got a friend to check the papers for stories of her, because he couldn't face what they might say. 'The newspapers don't say what a lovely person she is, what a caring girl she is, what a wonderful grandchild and child she has been to her parents,' he continued. 'All they will tell you is that she's a drug addict, that she's out of control. Of course that is partially true, but it's not the full truth. She's not really out of control, there are controls.'

There was a moment of relief, of a sort, in November, when Amy appeared at the MTV Europe Music Awards in Munich. She won the Brand New Artists' Choice award, an award introduced by MTV to allow other artists to vote for the act they rated most, while Mark Ronson again spoke up for his friend. 'As soon as I finish up the Daniel Merriweather record, I am going back into the studio with Amy Winehouse to work on her new record,' he reiterated. 'She is actually dying to go back into the studio already. She pretty much writes everything just on her acoustic guitar. When she's in her zone, she is just really clever and her lyrics are really special.'

But her actions were increasingly unprofessional. She had been due to turn up to a video shoot in London for

'Love Is A Losing Game', but never appeared, leaving the crew waiting all day for her – at an estimated cost of £70,000. This did not go down well. 'Amy was due on set first thing in the morning, but as the minutes ticked by she was nowhere to be seen,' said a source. 'People started panicking, but still gave it half an hour or so before calling her, but even then she wasn't picking up her mobile phone. Eventually someone got hold of her at 7pm and she said that she was still vegging out at home with her husband. Amy sounded a bit worse for wear as if she had been up all night. The crew weren't too impressed as they had set everything up – and they had to put up with the boredom of hanging around all day.' That was putting it mildly – other reports had it that some crew members had vowed never to work with the wayward star again.

Meanwhile, in the background, a problem had been lurking that was about to come to a head. Blake was due in court shortly on a charge of GBH, with the real chance of a prison sentence to come. He and his friend Michael Brown were accused of assaulting barman James King so badly he needed metal plates in his face after the attack. Some people were of the opinion that, if found guilty, a jail sentence would be no bad thing for Amy, in that it would force the troubled couple into a temporary separation, and give them the chance to actually sort out their problems.

'If Blake were to go to jail for GBH it would probably be the best thing that could happen for Amy,' Mitch said. 'It would give her a chance to recover and we could get her into rehab. She's got a long way to go in her recovery. She knows she's still got lots to sort out in her head. The trouble is, Blake seems to want them to go to rehab together and to be in control – and they've been told that isn't a good idea and that the likelihood of recovery is small. If he were in jail for a few months, assuming he was convicted, I think Amy would have a better chance of recovering. She needs to get herself sorted before she worries about him. She'd be mortified if he did go to jail, but it would be a real chance for her to get on the straight and narrow.'

Matters moved fast after that, and it looked very much as if Mitch was going to get what he wanted. There were reports that the police had raided the couple's home, while four men were arrested on suspicion of perverting the course of justice in relation to Blake's court case. Amy herself was not involved, and a spokesman was keen to say this had nothing to do with her usual problems: 'The only thing I can tell you is that it has nothing to do with drugs and that Amy is fine and she has not been charged or arrested,' he said.

Blake himself was one of those charged – he was pictured kissing Amy just before being led off in handcuffs – while a fifth man was arrested shortly afterwards in

Derbyshire. Amy herself was utterly hysterical. In tears, she said to the police, 'I want to go with him,' before crying to Blake, 'Baby, I love you. Baby I'll be fine.' A friend grabbed her and got her to come inside.

It was plain to the world quite how badly Amy was taking this: 'He would never try to fix his trial,' said Georgette Civil. 'It's just ridiculous. I know that and Amy knows that. Blake's been in custody all day. I managed to speak to him on the phone and he told me not to worry. Amy's totally distraught. She kept saying to me, "I love him. He's done nothing wrong". She was really upset because she couldn't go and visit him. Amy has told me she'll stand by Blake whatever happens.'

Mitch appeared to have changed his mind. 'I have no wish for him to go to prison as Amy and Blake are very much in love,' he said. The ever-loyal Mitch accompanied his daughter to Thames Magistrates' Court in east London, where Blake was remanded in custody, charged with conspiracy to pervert the course of justice. She blew him kisses and mouthed, 'I love you', as District Judge John Perkins presided over the proceedings. Blake was charged: 'That on or before the 8 November 2007, within the jurisdiction of the Central Criminal Court, you conspired together with James King, to do an act namely whereby James King would withdraw from being a witness in an indictment charged before the court against another for causing grievous bodily harm to James King with intent to pervert the course of justice contrary to Section One (1) of the Criminal Law Act 1977.'

His fellow defendant, Anthony Kelly, was charged 'with the attempt to pervert the course of public justice did a series of acts which had a tendency to pervert the course of public justice in that you arranged with the victim and the defendants in that the victim doesn't attend court.' James Kelly himself was also being charged.

Blake was carted off to Pentonville Prison, having been refused bail, while both families rallied round. The timing could not have been worse for Amy: she was about to start a UK tour. 'It will be difficult for her if Blake is not there, but she has got the boys in the band – she calls them her family – and us, her real family, to be there for her,' said her mother Janis. 'If he is jailed she will go through heartbreak but she will get over it because she is highly professional.' Unfortunately, that was not to prove totally accurate.

Meanwhile, Georgette Civil said that the families were sticking together: 'We've had our differences with Mitch, but we've agreed we have to fight this together.'

Janis was certainly optimistic to begin with. 'Amy not only needs to focus on the month ahead but re-focus on it,' she said. 'As her mother, I know she has got it in her to pull it off. She has also got me and her dad and the rest of the family around her and we'll be there for her. Amy has got to fix herself and with time she will. She has to go through a process but will come through it in time. And when we're able to get her back properly, she will be very much focused on her music and blossom still further. I have not spoken to her since police raided their home but Amy knows where to get in touch if she needs me. I've got faith in her and I am sure she will be out there on stage doing what she's so good at, making her fans happy. What she is experiencing at this moment is called life – where situations, sometimes unpleasant, present themselves, leaving you with the job of trying to overcome them.' They were wise words, but Janis had perhaps not realised quite how fragile her daughter had become. In truth, Amy was on the verge of collapse.

Shortly afterwards the trial was adjourned, as the GBH charge was now allied to attempting to pervert the course of justice. Amy was not at that hearing, not having been alerted to when it was being held, although Blake's mother was present. Amy did not appear to be doing very well on the outside. During an interview with the US magazine *Blender*, her behaviour verged on the bizarre: she started by saying she was no longer doing drugs as, 'I don't have time.' Was she an alcoholic? 'I don't know. I'm a really big drinker. I used to be there before the pub opened, banging on the door.' But what was really disconcerting was that she kept nodding off throughout the interview. 'What is wrong with me?' she asked after falling asleep in the middle of the interview. 'There's something wrong with me. I'm just really drowsy at the moment. I'm so sorry.'

Matters were not helped when Amy went to visit Blake at Pentonville and discovered that his mother Georgette had already taken the only permitted visit of the day. There were rumours that she and Blake's parents had fallen out. Far from Blake corrupting Amy, they seemed to be saying it was she who had got him into trouble and he was now paying the price.

'Things are very bad between Blake's and Amy's family,' said a friend. 'Amy is struggling to talk to his parents. When she turned up to see them on Sunday at the hotel where they have been staying, she was told first that they were asleep, then that they were not available. They are not taking any of her calls or being where they say they will be. Amy was devastated when she heard Blake's mum booked herself in for the jail visit, as Amy was desperate to see him. She just went to the prison anyway but was told she couldn't come in.'

And other friends were getting increasingly worried about how Amy really wasn't able to cope. 'Amy is in a real mess,' said one. 'It isn't pretty. When Blake first was arrested last Thursday she was strangely optimistic. It just didn't sink in. But seeing him in court on Saturday hit her really hard. She's been a mess since. One of her mates has not left her side to make sure she doesn't hurt herself.'

Mitch continued to express his concern. 'Blake only gets two prison visits a week,' he said. 'Amy has only managed to get one next week because his family are booking them all. Blake and I don't see eye to eye, but I will support him one million per cent – not being able to see your wife is inhumane. He can have up to three adults in a visit. We went on Wednesday with Amy but we couldn't go in. While she was in, I ran round to the front and booked her a visit in for Wednesday – otherwise she wouldn't be seeing him at all next week. Now she has to cope with seeing him only once – and that visit is shared with his family.'

The full extent of her decline became apparent when she started on the UK leg of her tour. The first concert was in Birmingham's National Indoor Arena, a show that was described by one reviewer as 'sometimes brilliant, but often shambolic'; it set the tone for what was to come. 'This is for my husband,' she informed the audience as prepared to sing 'Wake Up Alone', before rather unsteadily going on to other numbers. Her performance was such that there was booing; audience members started heading for the doors. 'To them people booing, wait till my husband gets out of incarceration,' yelled Amy. 'And I mean that.' Other antics included bumping into a guitar stand and dropping her microphone, before finally wandering off the stage all together. A success it was not.

In fact, opinions were sharply divided about the show. A number of people expressed sympathy with the problems Amy was going through, and pointed out that a star who had made herself famous by singing about refusing to go into rehab was never going to be the most clean cut of performers. Others, though, were furious, citing the cost of the tickets and a frankly shambolic performance. It was not what Amy needed in her current fragile state.

In the background, the court case rumbled on: now a sixth man was going to be charged. Blake's absence was taking an ever more public toll: it emerged that before the disastrous NEC concert, Amy had locked herself in the loo for half an hour, crying, 'I can't go on without Blake. How can I live without him? I need him. I need my baby.'

The omens weren't good. Amy flew to Scotland amidst scenes at the airport: looking pale and exhausted, she arrived surrounded by minders at Glasgow Airport, to play a gig at Barrowland. After heading in the wrong direction, she swore first at a bodyguard and then at the waiting crowd: it didn't look good. However, to everyone's surprise, this time she pulled it off: 'This is the second night of the tour, but it feels like the first,' she told the sell-out crowd, before coming out with a virtuoso performance. 'My husband is the best man in the world,' she told the audience, but this time there was no booing, only massive cheering. Her performance of 'Valerie' in Birmingham had been a disaster – she'd walked off halfway through – but this time there was no upset, merely a, 'Sorry, dad', when she was through.

The two sets of parents were still in disagreement – even within Amy's own family there was debate about whether or not Blake's incarceration was a good thing. Janis thought it was, as it would give Amy a chance to break free of her own addictions. 'Everyone else can see it, but Amy chooses not to,' she said. 'I think he introduced her to them [hard drugs] and now she thinks, "Oh, this is good, this is okay." I think she's still a child. Personally, I think it's overtaken her a bit. I step back, look at life, and think, "well, they've put him away". I can see life taking care of the situation. I was more worried when they were together. I think, while they are apart, she will wake up and think, "What have I done?" Again, it's a sense of fate. Thank God he's gone inside. Because it's also a case of "now he's going to learn".'

Not that she actually wanted the pair to split up. 'If the relationship is meant to be, it will survive this,' Janis continued. 'But Amy's got to love him for him, not because she feels sorry for him or because he's got her doped up – not for anything other than that she has respect for him.' She also thought Amy's sudden success might have a bearing on her problems. 'The music came too much, too soon, but her talent has turned on her,' she said. 'I hope Amy has not been taking drugs long enough for it to be a real addiction. I don't think she's stupid enough to actually keep going. Most people who are hooked on heroin don't have anything else in their life, but Amy has her music, her career, and a loving family.'

But by now her life had gone almost beyond soap-opera proportions. There were reports that her tour manager Thom Stone had angrily quit when drugs were found on the tour bus; shortly afterwards some crumpled tin foil, which could have been used for drug taking, was seen to be thrown out of her tour bus.

'Amy Winehouse boarded the bus outside Mar Hall Hotel at around 2:05pm,' said a passer-by, who had witnessed the whole event. 'Minutes later, I saw what I thought was a piece of rubbish being thrown out of the front door of the bus. I thought it was peculiar for something to be thrown out of the door, so after the bus pulled away I went over to investigate. It turned out to be some dirty cling film wrapped in tin foil. The foil looked to be charred and blackened as though it had been burned by a naked flame.'

Then there was the debate raging about her per-formances. Andrew Lloyd Webber had been present at the Birmingham concert and spoke up in her defense. 'My night in Birmingham was much enlivened by Ms Winehouse,' he said. 'I thought there were moments when she was absolutely magnificent. She came on stage announcing herself in true Judy Garland-style. I thought she handled herself very well.' Meanwhile the founder of Glastonbury, Michael Eavis, advised her to stop touring.

Another message of support came from one man Mitch was none too thrilled about: Pete Doherty. 'I speak to Amy almost every day,' he said. 'She just wants her man back for Christmas. They are desperately in love. One good thing is that Blake has got clean since he has been in prison. It's been quite an awakening. Amy stopped doing everything since he went in. She realises how much they have to lose. They are going to lose each other if it carries on. Love, music, and melody is the way forward.' They were wise words, but came from someone who seemed incapable of following them himself.

But Amy hadn't kicked her bad habits. She was pho-tographed with what appeared to be white powder in one nostril, a picture that elicited a great deal of criticism in the press. Shortly afterwards, she attended court to hear that Blake would be remanded in custody until the following January: the two mouthed messages of love and support to one another. Again, he was denied bail. Amy broke down in tears.

Alex Foden, Amy's hairdresser, had been offering a good deal of support and now revealed that Blake suggested she go away for Christmas. 'Amy told me Blake wants her to go away for Christmas to get away from it all,' he said. 'She is not on top of the world. But speaking to Blake on the phone helps. She'll go to Miami if Blake keeps going on about it, because she loves him and wants to make him happy.'

But she was falling apart. The tour had been continuing, with varying degrees of success, but in late November, Amy decided she couldn't take it any more. All the remaining dates on the tour were cancelled with immediate effect, just two hours before the next show was due to begin. 'Amy Winehouse has cancelled all remaining live and promotional appearances for the remainder of the year on the instruction of her doctor,' said a statement put out by Island Records. 'The rigours involved in touring and the intense emotional strain that Amy has been under in recent weeks have taken their toll. In the interests of her health and well-being, Amy has been ordered to take complete rest and deal with her health issues.'

Amy herself was in no doubt as to what was wrong.
'I can't give it my all on stage without my Blake,' she
said. 'I'm so sorry but I don't want to do the shows half-
heartedly; I love singing. My husband is everything to me
and without him it's just not the same.' This came shortly
after one of her most bizarre moments yet: after a show
in Brighton, in which quite a few of the audience walked
out, she ran from one hotel to another in the pouring rain,
shading her nose and picking at her teeth, before taking a
taxi back to London. It was clear she badly needed help.

Janis certainly welcomed the decision to cut the tour
short. 'Amy has got to take the opportunity of getting herself fitter and stronger,' she said. 'She thinks she is strong
but she isn't. I hope she uses the chance to fully recover. I
hope she will take it easy for a while and then get back to
writing new material. She has got to get herself clean. It is
a matter of her personal survival.'

Georgette felt the same way. 'I'm so relieved,' she
said. 'Cancelling is the best thing Amy could have done.
Now she can concentrate on getting better and keeping
her face clean. Amy needs to be left alone to get herself
together. We will try to lean on her to get her into rehab.
She knows she has to beat her drug addiction and now she
has a chance. We will persuade her to get the professional

help she needs. Amy was in pieces today. She doesn't want to let her fans down but she has no choice. She has to look after herself first.'

Georgette also revealed that Blake was writing Amy a series of notes to help her keep going. 'He wants her to feel as if they're still sharing life and he's with her every day,' she said. 'Blake thinks that if Amy has a little thing to do for him each day that'll propel her on, give her something to work towards, and get her out of bed in the morning.'

There was no sign of her immediately calming down. Just a couple of days after the tour was abandoned, she was pictured just outside her home, wearing only jeans and a bra. She looked completely traumatised and, indeed, there were suspicions that paparazzi waiting outside had somehow managed to get her to come out. Certainly, a friend said she'd only gone outside after hearing noises. 'She was sound asleep when she got up to check it out,' said a friend. 'She had spent the evening with a friend and thought he had come back because he had forgotten something. After being in a really deep sleep she had no idea what time it was – she just went outside to see what was going on. She didn't think it was necessary to get properly dressed as she was only going outside for a minute.'

Behind the scenes, the family sniping continued. 'She is using more cocaine and heroin,' snapped Georgette.

'She needs professional help.' Adding that Amy had only seen Blake in jail twice, she continued, 'I've had to help Amy to visit. She had no idea she can't just turn up too see Blake. What has she done to help him? Nothing.'

Given her problems, and the role Blake played in creating them, that was hardly surprising. Nor was her family thrilled at the amount of time she was spending with Pete Doherty. 'Everyone was hoping with Blake away in Pentonville Prison this would be a chance for Amy to get clean,' said a friend. 'But with Pete hanging around she has no chance. Mitch will be livid. He thinks Pete is a leech sucking the life out of Amy.'

She certainly didn't seem to be improving. One day she was seen wandering the streets at 4am; the next she missed a visit to Blake because she took so long to get ready. But despite all of this, there were signs that if only she could get over the many problems dragging her down, a brilliant career in the States could still be on the cards. She was nominated for no fewer than six Grammy awards in the United States for, amongst others, Best New Artist, Album of the Year, and Song of the Year for 'Rehab'. Only the rapper Kanye West, with eight, had more. Having been initially turned down for a US visa, she was now granted one, and so she would possibly be able to make the Grammy awards herself in February 2008 – as long as she managed to stay clean.

Amy At The Crossroads

AMY'S LIFE WAS at a crossroads. On the one hand, stunning global success could be hers had she the strength to give up her massively self-destructive lifestyle; on the other, she might let events overwhelm her. Her friends and family were on tenterhooks. A doctor was attending to her on a daily basis and Mitch, as ever, was at her side.

'Amy was visited by a doctor last night,' he told the *Daily Star* in early December. 'And we're seeing to it that she is monitored very carefully, every single day. So far, we're pleased with the way things are going. We are keeping a very close eye on her. We are all really pleased about the Grammy nominations, obviously. And we hope things will get better from now on. She must keep busy.'

Unfortunately matters were not improved when it emerged that Amy was to be quizzed by the police in connection with Blake's court case. 'We do want to talk to her about some matters, particularly financial ones, which may be important in this case,' said a source at Scotland Yard.

'It seems that in her marriage, she has been the breadwinner and has kept her husband in pocket money. We are trying to negotiate for her to come to see us, accompanied by her solicitor. We have been trying to do this for a while, but she has so far not been available.'

Concerned family and friends continued to rally around: there were plans to keep a close eye on her over Christmas, when Blake wouldn't be around. It also seemed that she would be liable for his legal bill, as Blake was denied legal aid, with the cost to date standing at about £300,000. An enraged Mitch exploded anew, especially at Georgette. 'Amy is going to pay for his legal team and that will be a lot of money,' he said. 'I don't see how anyone can say she's not doing anything for him. His mother hasn't been forthcoming with an offer to put her hand in her pocket, so maybe she should keep her opinions to herself. Blake has been doing better. He has got character and has shown maturity while he's been away and I like that. I think that's good. But, by the same token, his problems were there long before he met Amy. Blake's mother seems to want to blame the whole world – everyone apart from herself.'

He also explained that Amy was still extremely down. 'It's clear there are issues of self-image, self-loathing,' he said. 'We were recently looking at photos of her five years ago, when she was curvy, and she said, "I look really happy there". I said, "Aren't you happy now, darling?" And she said, "I've been happier". There was a realisation there. I know the real problem is that she's depressed about Blake being in prison.'

It wasn't looking good and matters worsened still when Amy was arrested in connection with the alleged plot to pervert the cause of justice. She spent a couple of hours being quizzed by police at Shoreditch police station in east London – Mitch and a lawyer were in attendance – while the police put out a statement. 'A twenty-four-year-old woman has been released on police bail to return to an East London police station on a date in early March next year,' said a spokeswoman for Scotland Yard.

Amy herself put out a dignified statement. 'She attended a police station voluntarily and at a pre-agreed time' said her spokesman. 'She was arrested, but that is common practice for someone being interviewed by police. There have been no charges and she has been released.'

Mitch was also keen to make the situation clear. 'It had all been arranged weeks in advance,' he said. 'The only way the police could take a DNA sample was if Amy was under arrest. Apart from the police visit, Amy is doing well and we're all pleased with her progress as far as her getting better is concerned. She still needs to rest and that's exactly what she'll be doing over the next few weeks.'

There were concerns, as well, that Amy might have some kind of wish to go to prison, in order to find herself in the same position as Blake. 'It's almost like she would want that – so she would be feeling how Blake feels,' said a friend. 'Everyone is trying to get her to snap out of it but we worry for her. The past few weeks have been hard on her and we don't want to see her self-destruct but she's been on a downward spiral for a while.'

Georgette didn't seem to think so, again speaking out against her wayward daughter-in-law. 'When Amy's out all night, she can't get up the next day and keeps missing prison visits,' she said. 'Blake can't dictate to Amy but he gets upset when she forgets to visit or turns up too late and is turned away. I have to ring her sometimes six times a day to remind her to get up, get washed, and get over there.'

Amy soldiered on. She was also planning to appear in court in Norway again, to challenge her drug conviction. Belatedly, she and her people had realised this might limit her ability to tour the world, and so were intent on getting it overturned.

And there were reports that Blake was increasingly un-happy in jail. 'Blake is like a lost soul in there,' said a former inmate, who had met him inside. 'He is very frightened and he does not know what he's doing. I spent a night in a cell with him on G wing in Pentonville. He was working in the kitchens and we chatted about stuff. He said he loved Amy dearly and that he wanted to start a family with her. He also seemed to enjoy the fact she had got so many tattoos and that many of them were dedicated to him. He was in a strange old state and said he was cracking up. One day I was down talking to my solicitor and Blake was in another room. Amy had to come to visit him in private because she is so high profile. The door was shut but I could hear Blake shout, "Just fucking get me out of here!" He was desperate to get out and can't believe how he's got into this situation.'

Despite all this, Amy's career remained on track – other than the touring aspect of it, that is. 'Valerie' was doing well in the charts, and Amy remained massively in demand all over the world. There was a real sense that if she could only pull it together, the world could be hers for the taking.

Christmas was quiet and shortly afterwards, Amy flew to Mustique, to stay in the rock star Bryan Adams's villa on the island. It was a much-needed break. 'Amy has got stronger and healthier in the last two weeks and the holiday should help too.' said Mitch. 'She has refused to be admitted into rehab but, hopefully, the break will mean rehab goes to her. She has started treatment and this will continue on holiday. I'd have liked to be with her, but she didn't want her old dad around.'

Adams himself was very sympathetic to Amy's plight – as was his Mustique neighbour Mick Jagger. 'He is keen to help her,' said a friend. 'Mick could join them. He has also said he wants to help Amy.'

And the merry go round that is her life continued to spin. One story doing the rounds was that as soon as Blake was free, the two of them would be trying for a baby. 'On her last prison visit she told Blake she wants to try to get pregnant as soon as she can,' said a friend. 'She reckons it would pull them together as a family and help them focus their lives on something positive. It sounds like a crazy idea, but on the other hand it could be the thing that adds stability to her life. Amy is really hopeful he will be allowed out and that they can get on with their lives. But one of the first things she wants to do is hit the bedroom and make her latest plan come true. Amy has her mind set on it and will do all she can to make it happen.'

There were also reports of a falling out with Pete Doherty, because he made the serious mistake of trying to woo her. Amy was as besotted with Blake as she ever had been, and so the likelihood of her saying yes was always low and, in fact, she became very upset.

Yet another report had Blake and Amy planning to renew their wedding vows. Amy had already written a song for Blake called 'For You', and it seemed she wanted to go one step further still in her declaration of love. 'When Blake was first arrested, they both declared their undying love for each other and promised each other it'd be good to renew their vows,' said a friend. 'And the time feels right to do that now. They are missing each other terribly. Amy wants them to repeat the same vows they took when they originally tied the knot in a £60 ceremony in Miami last May.'

At the time of writing, it seems that Amy will not face criminal charges in relation to Blake's court case, and she is, at least, clearly aware that if her career is to continue, she must change her ways. The attempt to overturn the drugs conviction is a highly positive sign, as at least it shows she still has the will to tour worldwide, and that she is looking to the future. New material is beginning to emerge and her enforced separation from Blake may save her yet.

But whatever happens to her next, Amy's story has been a remarkable one. For a young girl growing up in north London to turn so suddenly into a major star is a story that comes along only a couple of times with every generation. Of Amy's talent, there is no doubt: she is the freshest and most original voice to hit the music scene in years.

And if she does overcome her personal problems, there is no doubt that she will be around for decades. Nor, in the longer term, will they necessarily have done her too much harm. The music business is one of the toughest in the world in which to survive, and Amy has so far done just that, coping with problems that would have floored a lesser person. Her body may look fragile, but for all that, there is steel at the core.

And Amy Winehouse has been a phenomenon. She's a tiny woman with a huge talent; a very young Jewish girl from London who sounds like a forty-something black torch-singer from Harlem. Her career has been pretty extraordinary. But then – so is her voice.